THE
EVERYTHING®
GUITAR SCALES
BOOK

Dear Reader,

I remember it fondly. My older brother had just gone away for a semester abroad, leaving his guitar behind. Being the upstanding younger brother I was, I totally ignored his wishes to "leave my guitar alone" and ran up and grabbed the instrument as soon as he was out the door. What I do remember is that the first thing I did was play up and down one string. I found a bunch of frets that sounded good together. When I ran upstairs and played along to the radio (Metallica's "Fade to Black"), I was amazed that each of the notes I had found sounded good—I had discovered a scale, but I didn't know it yet. As I kept playing, I found more and more of these patterns that worked over every song I listened to. As I kept going, I saw patterns emerge all over the neck, and I knew that I was hooked. I really loved the sound of those scales, and I loved to create melodies and solos with them.

As I grew up, I learned about music and began to understand the great significance of scales in every aspect of music. As a professional musician, scales are something that I use on a daily basis in my music. I think you could spend your whole life studying this stuff and never get bored—I never have. There are literally millions of scales, but I've distilled this down the to scales that I think come up most often in professional music (across all genres). Don't worry if you don't get to them right away. Take what you need, and come back for more when you're ready. You'll bring your own music and musicianship to each scale, which is just a bunch of dots on a paper, but your own creativity will bring them to life. I wish you the best of luck on your journey.

Warmly,

Welcome to the EVERYTHING® Series!

These handy, accessible books give you all you need to tackle a difficult project, gain a new hobby, comprehend a fascinating topic, prepare for an exam, or even brush up on something you learned back in school but have since forgotten.

You can choose to read an *Everything*® book from cover to cover or just pick out the information you want from our four useful boxes: e-questions, e-facts, e-alerts, and e-ssentials. We give you everything you need to know on the subject, but throw in a lot of fun stuff along the way, too.

We now have more than 400 *Everything*® books in print, spanning such wide-ranging categories as weddings, pregnancy, cooking, music instruction, foreign language, crafts, pets, New Age, and so much more. When you're done reading them all, you can finally say you know *Everything*®!

PUBLISHER Karen Cooper

DIRECTOR OF ACQUISITIONS AND INNOVATION Paula Munier

MANAGING EDITOR, EVERYTHING SERIES Lisa Laing

COPY CHIEF Casey Ebert

ACQUISITIONS EDITOR Lisa Laing

DEVELOPMENT EDITOR Brett Palana-Shanahan

EDITORIAL ASSISTANT Hillary Thompson

MUSIC ENGRAVER Marc Schonbrun

Visit the entire Everything® series at *www.everything.com*

THE
EVERYTHING®
GUITAR SCALES
BOOK
with CD

Over 700 scale patterns for every style of music

Marc Schonbrun

Avon, Massachusetts

This book is dedicated to every musician and
teacher who's ever made a difference in my life. There
are too many to mention, but most of you know who you are already.

An Everything® Series Book.
Everything® and everything.com® are registered trademarks of F+W Media, Inc.

Published by Adams Media, a Division of F+W Media, Inc.
57 Littlefield Street, Avon, MA 02322 U.S.A.
www.adamsmedia.com

ISBN 10: 1-59869-574-6
ISBN 13: 978-1-59869-574-8

Printed in the United States of America.

J   I   H   G   F   E   D   C   B

Library of Congress Cataloging-in-Publication Data
available from the publisher

This publication is designed to provide accurate and authoritative information with regard to the subject matter covered. It is sold with the understanding that the publisher is not engaged in rendering legal, accounting, or other professional advice. If legal advice or other expert assistance is required, the services of a competent professional person should be sought.

—From a *Declaration of Principles* jointly adopted by a Committee of the American Bar Association and a Committee of Publishers and Associations

Many of the designations used by manufacturers and sellers to distinguish their products are claimed as trademarks. Where those designations appear in this book and Adams Media was aware of a trademark claim, the designations have been printed with initial capital letters.

This book is available at quantity discounts for bulk purchases.
For information, please call 1-800-289-0963.

Contents

Introduction / 1

1 The Pentatonic Scales / 7
The Major Pentatonic Scale in All Twelve Keys / 8
The Minor Pentatonic Scale in All Twelve Keys / 20

2 The Major Scale / 32
The Major/Ionian Scale in All Twelve Keys / 33

3 The Minor Scale / 45
The Minor/Aeolian Scale in All Twelve Keys / 46

4 The Special Minor Scales / 58
The Harmonic Minor Scale in All Twelve Keys / 59
The Melodic Minor Scale in All Twelve Keys / 71

5 The Dorian Scale / 83
The Dorian Scale in All Twelve Keys / 84

6 The Phrygian Scale / 96
The Phrygian Scale in All Twelve Keys / 97

7 The Lydian Scale / 109
The Lydian Scale in All Twelve Keys / 110

8 The Mixolydian Scale / 122
The Mixolydian Scale in All Twelve Keys / 123

9 The Locrian Scale / 135
The Locrian Scale in All Twelve Keys / 136

10 The Whole-Tone Scale / 148
The Whole-Tone Scale in All Twelve Keys / 149

11 The Diminished Scales / 161
The Half-Whole Diminished Scale in All Twelve Keys / 162
The Whole-Half Diminished Scale in All Twelve Keys / 174

12 Jazz/Modern Scales / 186
The Bebop Dominant Scale in All Twelve Keys / 187
The Major Bebop Scale in All Twelve Keys / 199
The Altered Dominant Scale in All Twelve Keys / 212
The Locrian ♯2 Scale in All Twelve Keys / 224
The Mixolydian ♯4 Scale in All Twelve Keys / 237

Acknowledgments

I need to acknowledge my family for all that they do for me—their support is absolutely incredible.

Deep thanks go to Jeff Rosenbluth, who showed me that working smarter always beats working harder—Jeff, you have helped me so much, and I can't even think of a way to thank you.

Finally, thanks to Doug Rubio for taking a chance on me. You never should have let me into the Crane School of Music, but I'm so glad that you did. You got this whole thing started—I continue to absorb, utilize, and cherish what I learned from you.

Introduction

▶ WELCOME TO *The Everything® Guitar Scales Book with CD*. The purpose of this book is to show you all the possibilities of musical scales that exist on the guitar. This book is intended to be a complete reference to how to play, understand, and find scales in every key, in every position on your guitar. To facilitate this, you'll spend most of your time looking at guitar fingerboard grids—you won't need to learn to read a note of music. Each visual diagram will tell you exactly where to place your fingers, which fingers to use, and the name of each scale.

The book is organized by the type of scales with each scale shown in all twelve keys, in four different locations on the guitar's fingerboard. You'll find scales for every situation, sound, and mood you can imagine. Though you'll learn some basics about what makes scales what they are, this book is focused on the scale shapes themselves, and not the theory behind him. Think of this as an application guide, rather than an explanation into the "why." If you're interested in the theory behind scales, you'll find other books from the "Everything" series to your liking, especially *The Everything® Reading Music Book* and *The Everything® Music Theory Book*.

What Is a Scale?

A scale is simply an organization of music notes or tones. There are literally thousands of scales if you start combining all twelve chromatic notes from the musical alphabet together in various ways. What you'll learn in this book is a great collection of useful scales to get you through just about every musical situation you can imagine. Within each section, you'll learn some important info about the scale in question, what style(s) of music utilize that scale, and, where applicable, which chords correlate with those scales.

For the purposes of this book, a scale is defined as musical material that you can use to create melodies, whether composed or improvised. You can make riffs and hooks with them, and as your knowledge of scales grows deeper, you can learn to make chords and harmony from these scales. No guitarist gets through even his first month of guitar lessons without learning at least one scale! This book will outline the following nineteen scales:

- Major pentatonic
- Minor pentatonic
- Major
- Minor
- Harmonic minor
- Melodic minor
- Dorian
- Phrygian
- Lydian
- Mixolydian
- Locrian
- Whole tone
- Half whole diminished
- Whole half diminished
- Dominant bebop
- Major bebop
- Altered dominant
- Locrian ♯2
- Mixolydian ♯4

Since each scale is detailed in all twelve musical keys, and each scale has four locations on the fingerboard to work with, you'll have access to over 930 different scale patterns. You'll never run out of ideas!

Theory

Before you see any of the scales, you'll see a bit of background information on the scale. One of the things you'll see is a sample of the musical notes contained within the scale. In each case, you'll see this in relation to the C scale only (rather than all twelve chromatic spellings). This is to serve as a reference for you. You'll also see the *scale degrees,* which is a way of identifying the scale tones by numbers. As you get more interested in music theory, and you check out *The Everything® Music Theory Book,* you'll see scale degrees referenced often. Knowing the scale degrees, coupled with knowledge of key signatures, will allow you to spell all the notes in any scale you see in this book.

How to Read the Visual Diagrams

In this book, you'll see an overview of the guitar's fingerboard with dots/fingerings placed on the neck to indicate where to press. Let's start with a blank diagram (Figure 1) and explain what you're looking at.

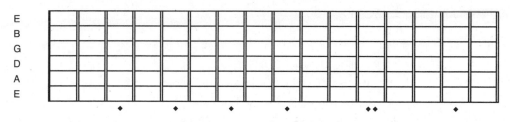

Figure 1: Blank fretboard diagram

Each fretboard contains six strings, just like your guitar. To the left of the scale are the following notes:

- E
- B
- G
- D
- A
- E

These notes correspond to the names of the open strings of the guitar. With that said, the diagrams are laid out with the low strings on the bottom of the diagrams and the high strings on the top of the diagrams. If you set your guitar in your lap, with the fingerboard up, you'll be looking down at the fretboard diagram you'll see throughout this book.

Below each diagram is a group of what look like diamonds. These diamonds are located at the following frets:

- 3rd fret
- 5th fret
- 7th fret
- 9th fret
- 12th fret (double diamonds)
- 15th fret

Each of these diamonds corresponds to the typical position markers that you find inlaid into your fingerboard. Most guitars have them as circles, but some have more ornate shapes (and many of them diamonds). In any case, they are there to help you find your way on the fretboard. On the diagrams in this book, you'll see them on the bottom of the fingerboard because you'll need to keep the actual fingerboard free for the notes you'll play. The diamonds are there to show you on which fret the scale shape will occur.

The fretboard diagram itself is a grid of 6 × 16 boxes, with each box designating a fret. This diagram provides a simple explanation of how to read the diagrams. (See Figure 2.)

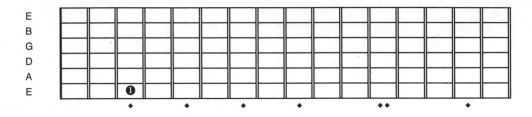

Figure 2: Example scale

This scale isn't really a scale, but it does provide us a great way to illustrate how the system works. The single dot (in this case a 1) is on the bottom row, on the lowest space, which designates that it's the sixth string. The dot is placed on the 3rd fret (also designated by a diamond). Press down the third fret of the sixth string, and you'll have read your first diagram.

Full Diagrams

Now that you understand how the diagrams are put together, let's look at a sample scale. (See Figure 3.)

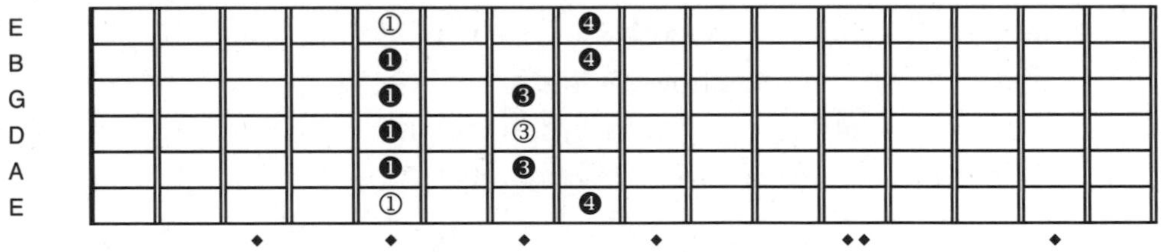

Figure 3: A minor pentatonic scale

You can see that this scale has two notes on each string and that every string is used (which is consistent throughout this book). How do you play this? This is the fun part! A scale has no start and no end. A scale is just showing you what you *can* play to make the sound of A minor pentatonic happen. There is no right, or wrong way, to play it. It's analogous to an alphabet. You can make words as you please and organize them into sentences. What a scale is *not* is a rote pattern that you'll ever play the same way twice. Think of each scale in this book as a vast array of possibilities. Mix them up, play them out of order, skip around. The more you experiment, the more fun you'll have, and the more original your solos and riffs will sound.

The Dots

Throughout this book, there are dots placed on the fingerboard to indicate which fingers you should use. Firstly, the fingerings are merely a suggestion. You'll find that the fingerings in this book are there to make your life as a player easier. But if at any point you feel that you have figured out a better fingering, please don't hesitate to use it—only the sound of the scale comes through to the listener, not the fingers used!

You'll see two different color dots in the diagrams: black and white. The black dots are the majority of the markings on the scale diagrams. They tell you what finger to press, and where to play them; their color is arbitrary. On the other hand, the white dots indicate the root of the scale. (For instance, if you're playing a C major scale, all of the Cs will be in white.) This will help you learn the notes on your fingerboard as you progress throughout the book. Since all of the scales in this book progress in more than one octave, you'll see more than one white circle (indicating the root). This will give you a chance to anchor the root of the scale from more than one place on your neck, greatly speeding up your learning of the notes on the fingerboard—a task that every guitarist should take seriously!

A Sample Page

Let's look at a sample page, so you can see what you'll encounter. Figure 4, on page 6 shows the C major scale that you'll find within this book.

What you're looking at is four different variations of the same scale. Each scale pattern contains the exact same pitches (C, D, E, F, G, A, B, C). What each diagram shows you is how to play those same pitches, and more importantly, the sounds of those scales in a few spots on your neck. You can start in any position on the neck you choose and go back and forth as you please. Think of them, once again, as a set of possibilities.

How This Book Is Organized

This book is organized into twelve chapters. Each chapter contains one particular sound. There's a chapter for major scales, and another chapter for diminished scales. Within each chapter, you'll get some brief introductory text telling you about the musical formula behind the scale, where you'll commonly use those scales (stylistically), some famous songs and melodies based on those scales, and, when applicable, which chords are associated with those scales. Directly following that information will be your scale diagrams. Each scale will be listed in every key, so each scale will take up twelve pages, with

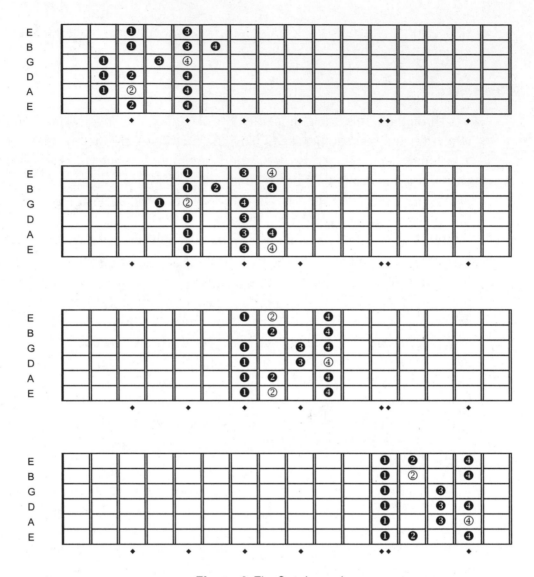

Figure 4: The C major scale

one page for each chromatic key. This will make this book a complete, easy-to-use reference. You'll just find the chapter you want, and all the scales will be right there. Just pick the part of the neck you'd like to play in, and you'll see every possible note in front of you.

Also within each chapter is a link to the accompanying audio CD. For each of the nineteen scales within the book, there is a musical example so you can hear what the scale sounds like. You're not expected to know all the scales in the book, and that's the fun! You're going to learn some great new sounds, and the CD will help your ear acclimate to the new, and sometimes unusual, timbres.

And without further delay, you're probably itching to get to the scales, so here you go!

CHAPTER 1

The Pentatonic Scales

No scale is more closely tied to guitar than the pentatonic scale, which you will learn in two varieties: major and minor. Pentatonic simply means "five tone," so throughout musical history, there have been many pentatonic scales. The two you'll learn are the most standard pentatonic scales. No mater what style of music you play, you're going to play the pentatonic scales!

The Major Pentatonic Scale in All Twelve Keys

The major pentatonic scale is a five-note scale, which in the key of C would contain the notes (C, D, E, G, A), which are also the scale degrees of (1, 2, 3, 5, 6). The major pentatonic scale is immensely popular in practically all genres of music. It's particularly prevalent in folk, bluegrass, country, and rock. You'd use this scale when playing over major chord progressions, or major chord vamps. It's a lovely scale that's hard to make sound bad.

The Minor Pentatonic Scale in All Twelve Keys

There is no scale more important to guitarists than the minor pentatonic scale. The minor pentatonic scale in the key of C would contain the notes C, E♭, F, G, B♭, which are the scale degrees of 1, ♭3, 4, 5, ♭7. This scale is used in every genre of music, and is the sound of rock 'n' roll and the blues. You'll be hard pressed to find a scale more widely used than the minor pentatonic scale.

C Major Pentatonic

The Major Pentatonic Scale

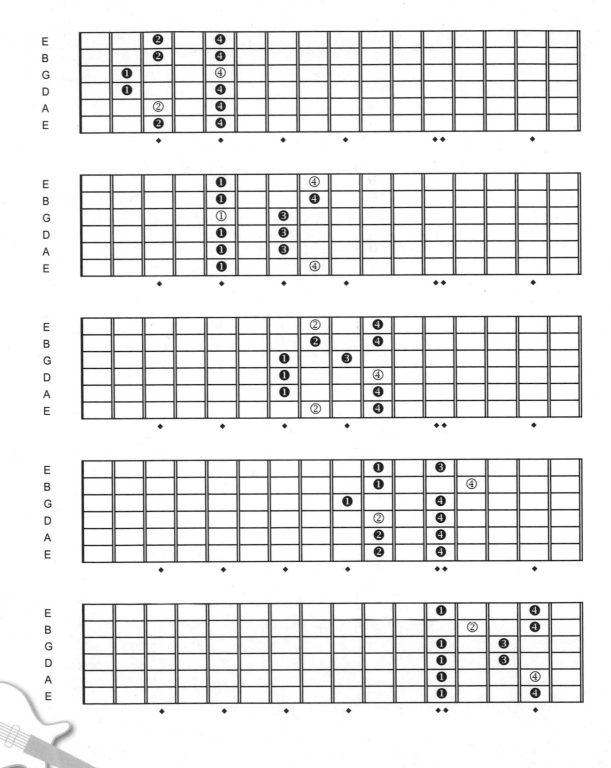

C#/D♭ Major Pentatonic

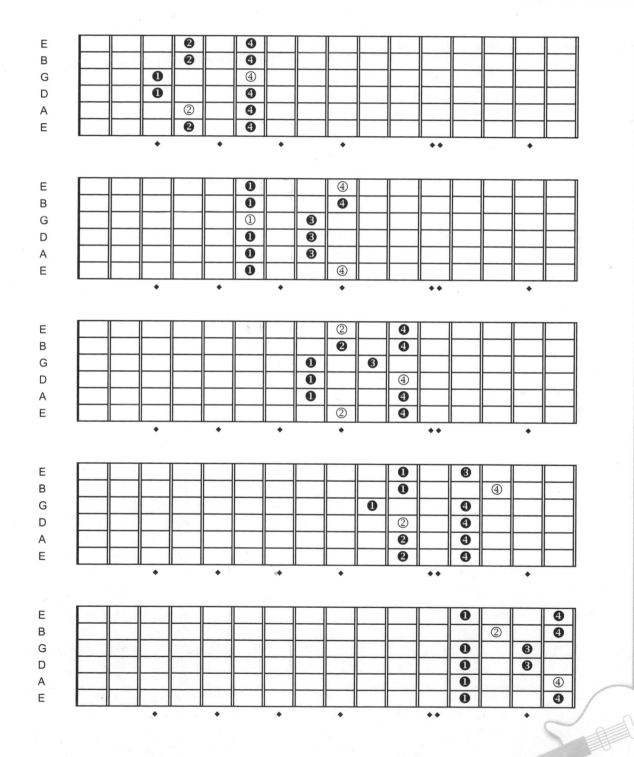

D Major Pentatonic

The Major Pentatonic Scale

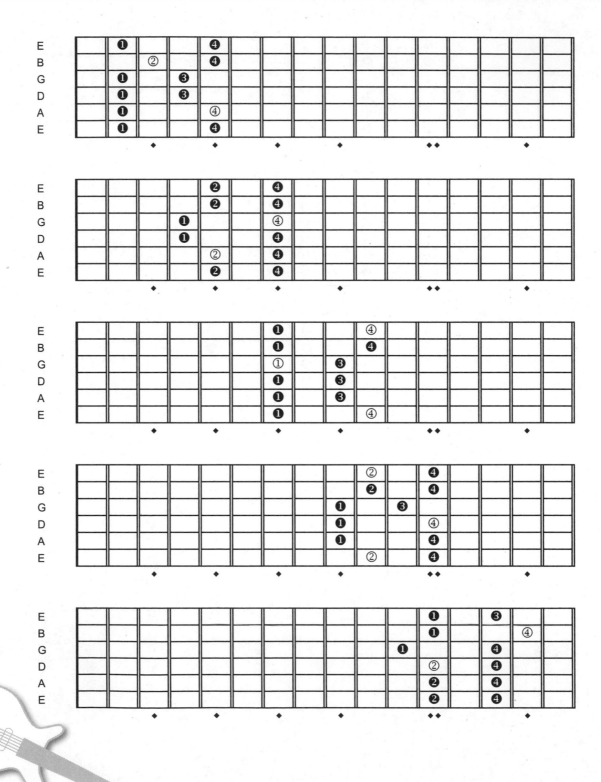

D♯/E♭ Major Pentatonic

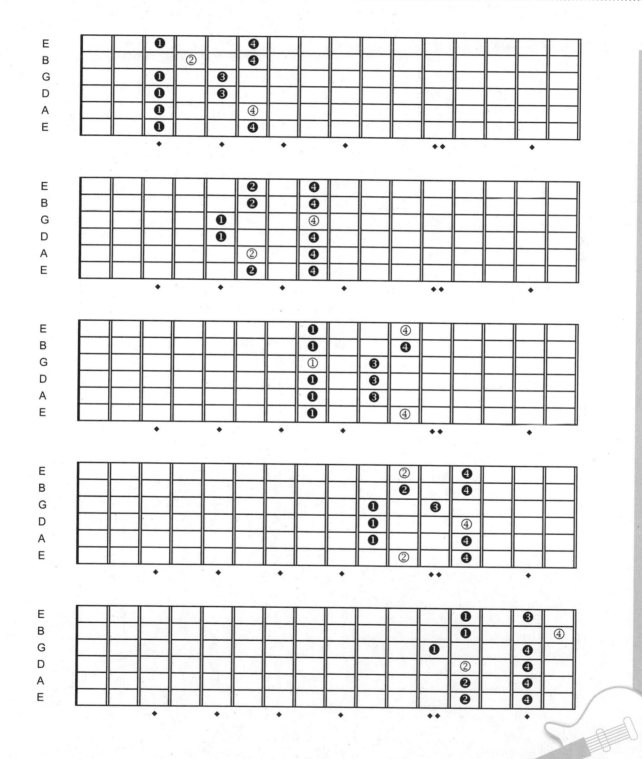

The Major Pentatonic Scale

Track 1

E Major Pentatonic

The Major Pentatonic Scale

F Major Pentatonic

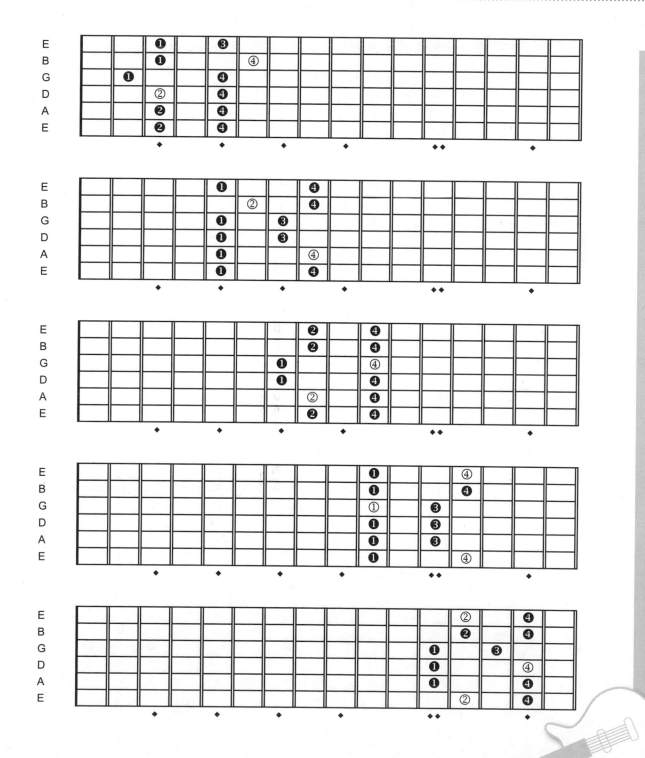

F♯/G♭ Major Pentatonic

The Major Pentatonic Scale

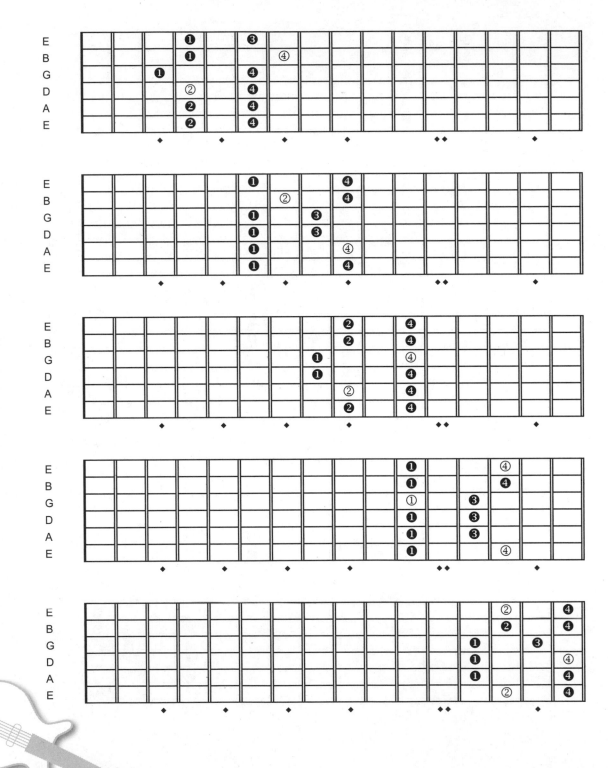

G Major Pentatonic

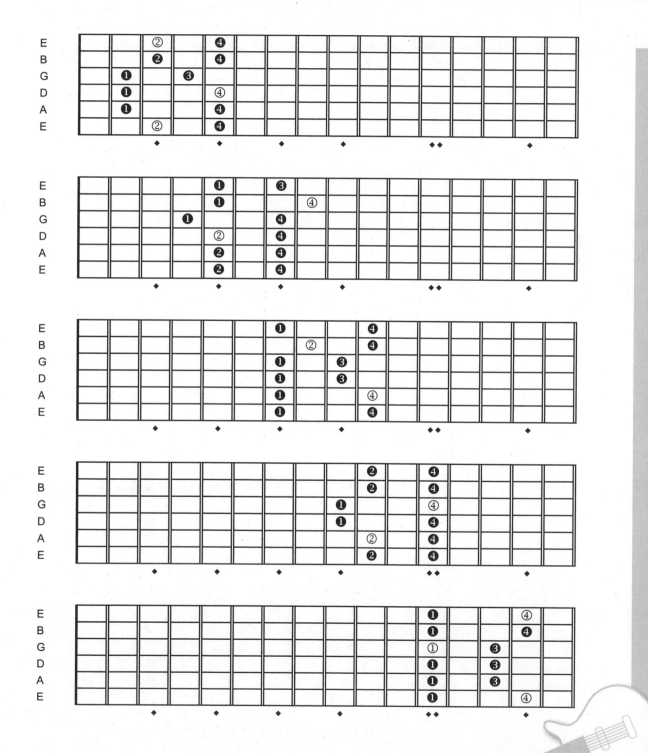

The Major Pentatonic Scale

G#/A♭ Major Pentatonic

The Major Pentatonic Scale

A Major Pentatonic

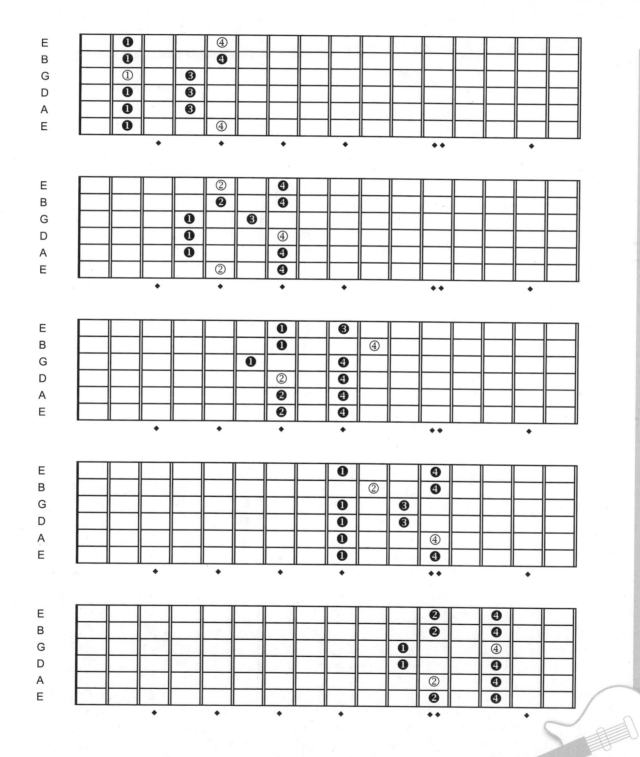

The Major Pentatonic Scale

A#/B♭ Major Pentatonic

The Major Pentatonic Scale

B Major Pentatonic

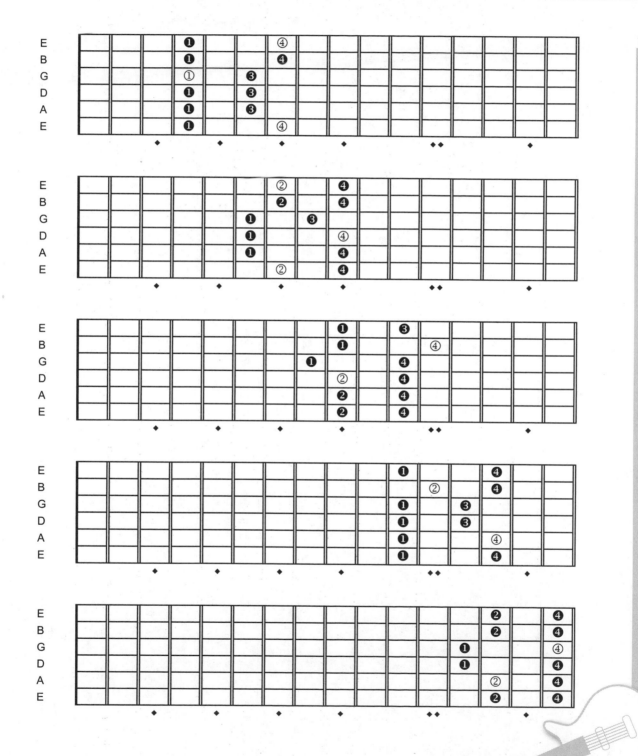

C Minor Pentatonic

The Minor Pentatonic Scale

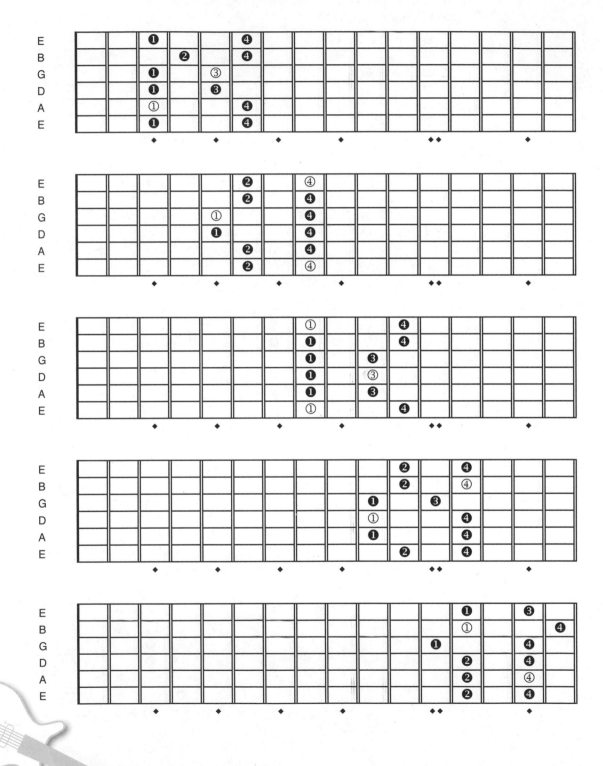

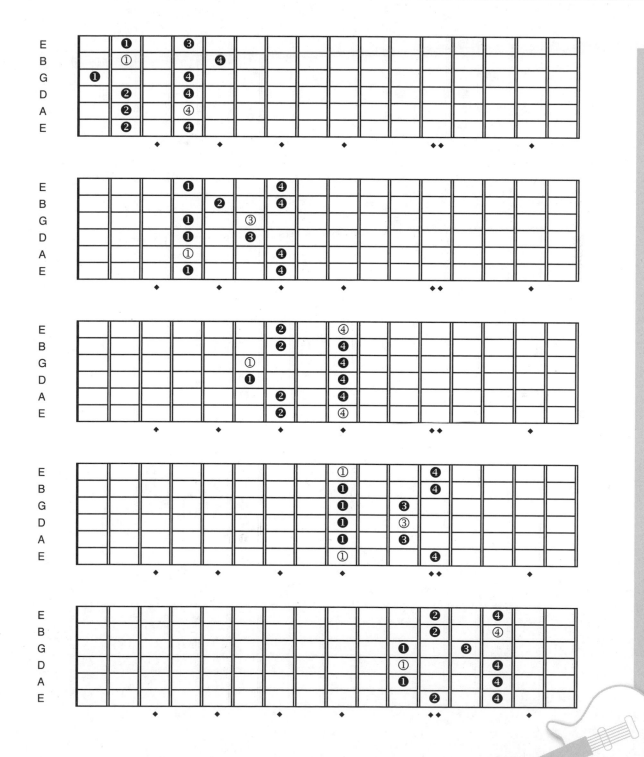

C#/D♭ Minor Pentatonic

The Minor Pentatonic Scale

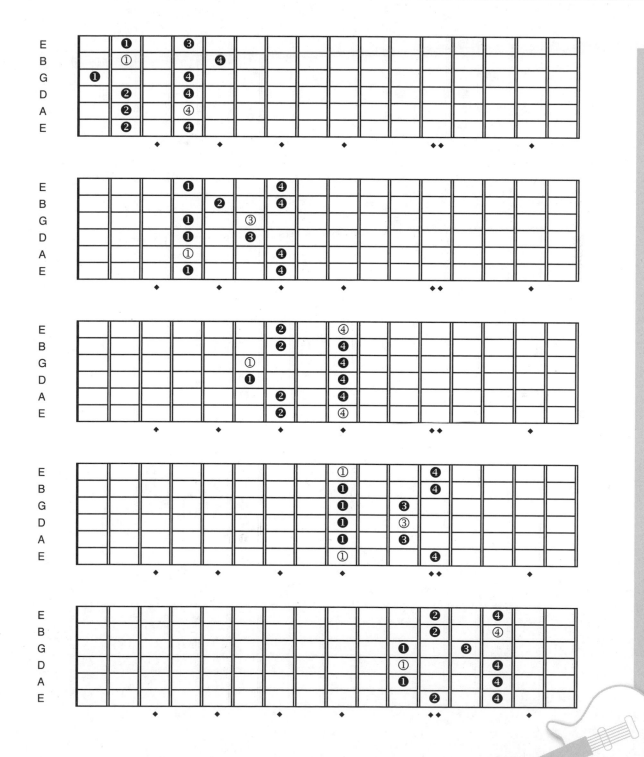

D Minor Pentatonic

The Minor Pentatonic Scale

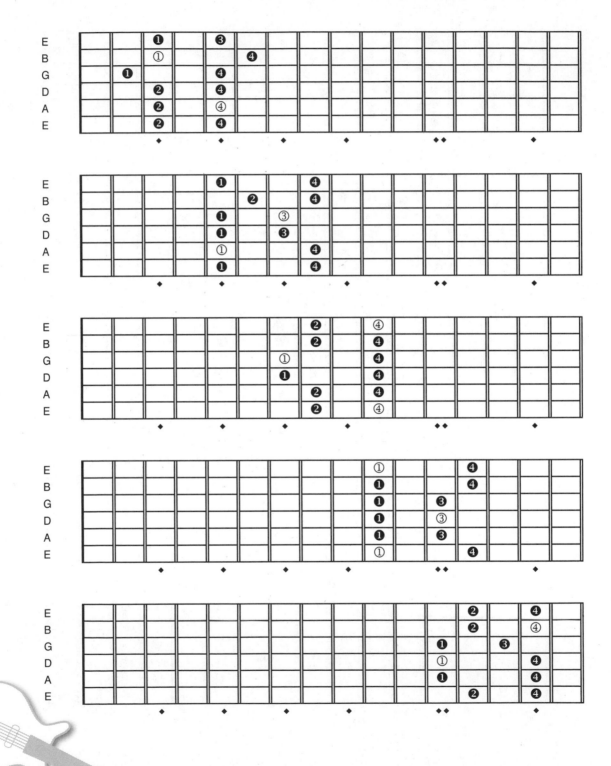

D#/E♭ Minor Pentatonic

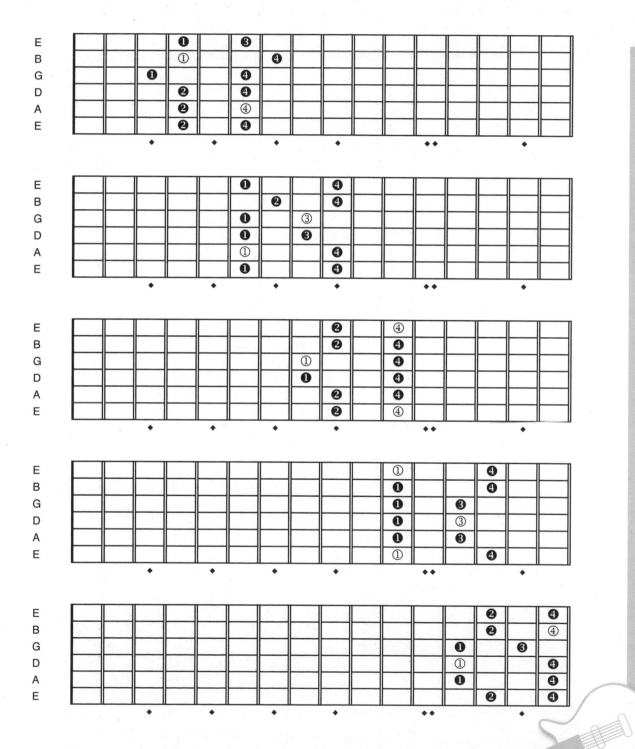

The Minor Pentatonic Scale

Track 2

E Minor Pentatonic

The Minor Pentatonic Scale

F Major Pentatonic

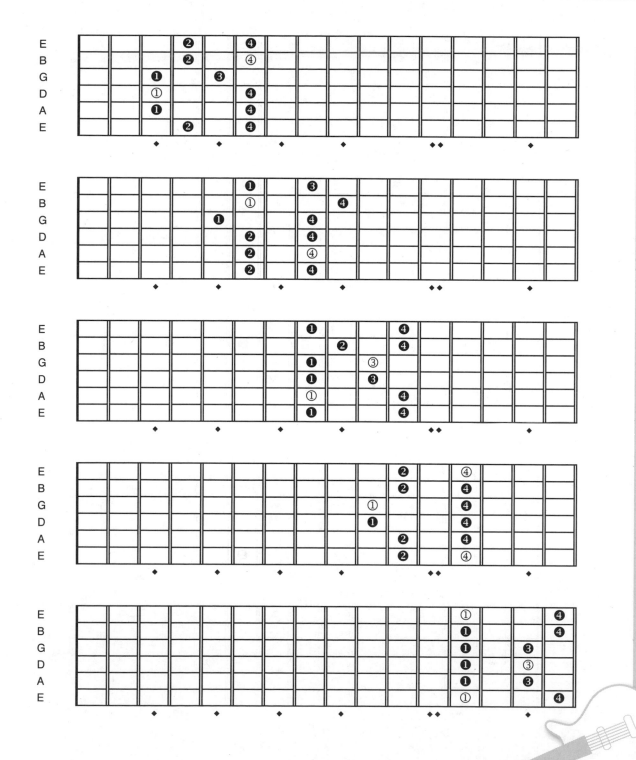

The Minor Pentatonic Scale

F#/G♭ Minor Pentatonic

The Minor Pentatonic Scale

G Minor Pentatonic

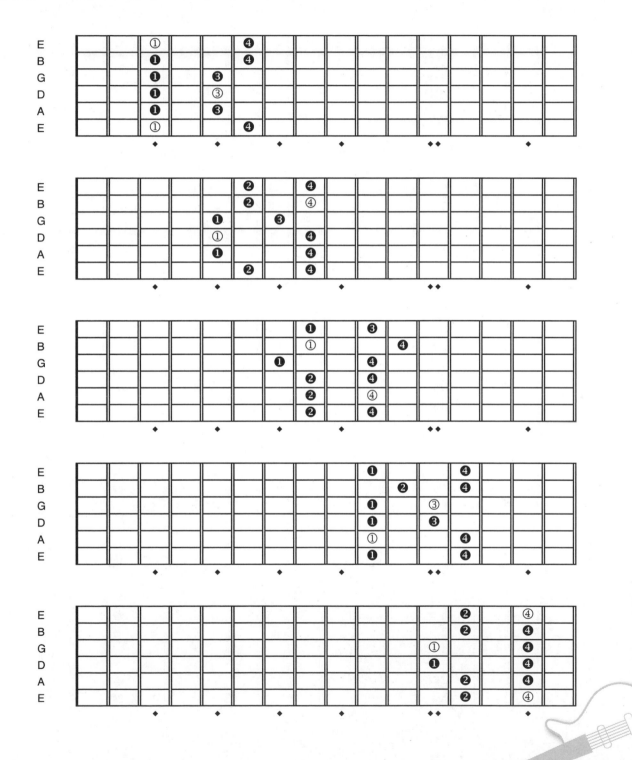

The Minor Pentatonic Scale

G#/A♭ Minor Pentatonic

The Minor Pentatonic Scale

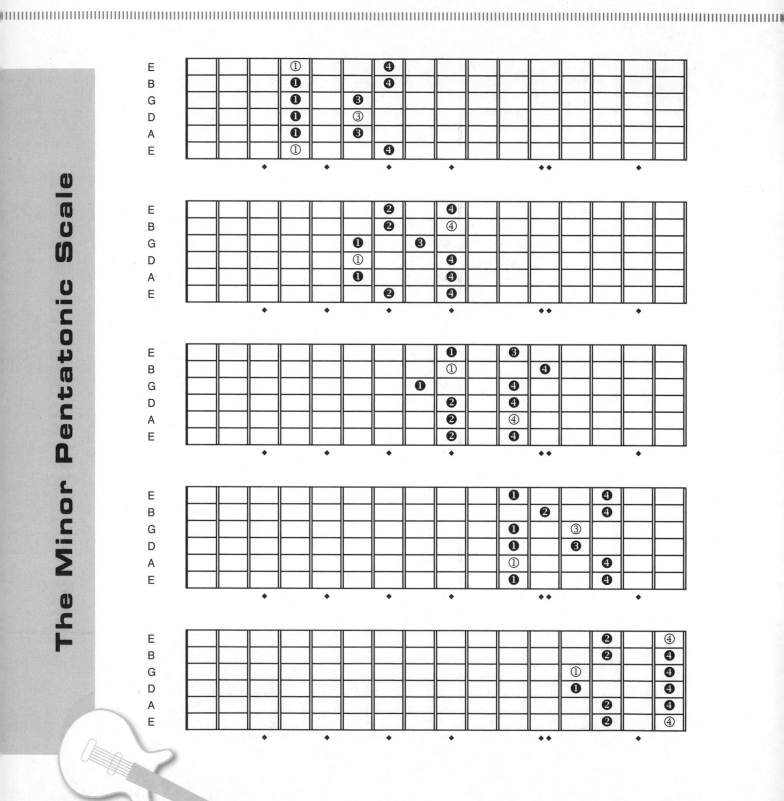

A Minor Pentatonic

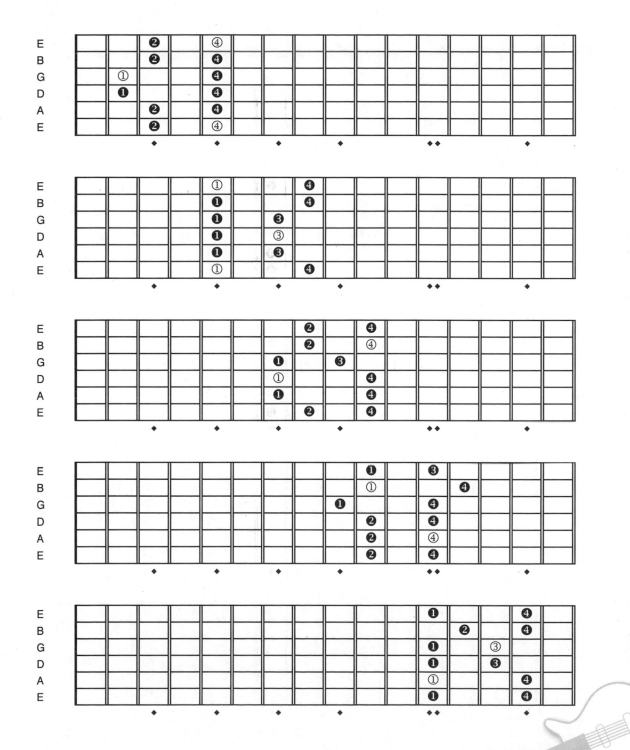

A♯/B♭ Minor Pentatonic

The Minor Pentatonic Scale

B Minor Pentatonic

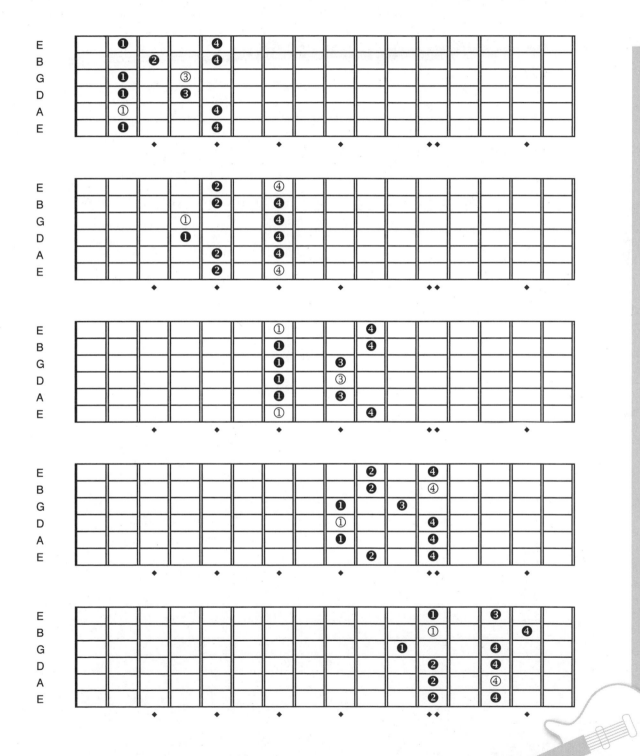

CHAPTER 2

The Major Scale

For musicians, the beginning of music theory starts with the major scale. This seven-note scale is one of the underpinnings of traditional harmony and is a great resource for melodies. The major scale is thousands of years old, and you'll find it in literally all genres of music. Being able to play major scales could well be your first step into music theory and to unlocking your guitar.

The Major/Ionian Scale in All Twelve Keys

The major scale in C would spell as C, D, E, F, G, A, B, C. Since every scale in this book relates to the major scale, its scale degrees are 1, 2, 3, 4, 5, 6, 7. This scale has ties to the old church modes, which originate from the Greek music system. Due to this fact, you'll see this scale referred to as "the major scale" and as "the Ionian mode." Either way, it's the same scale.

The major scale is used for soloing and creating melodies in major keys. You hear it in virtually every style of music, and it's got that calming, yet happy feeling when you play it. It's also a staple of classical music melodies, so don't be surprised if you accidentally find some familiar melodies!

C Major

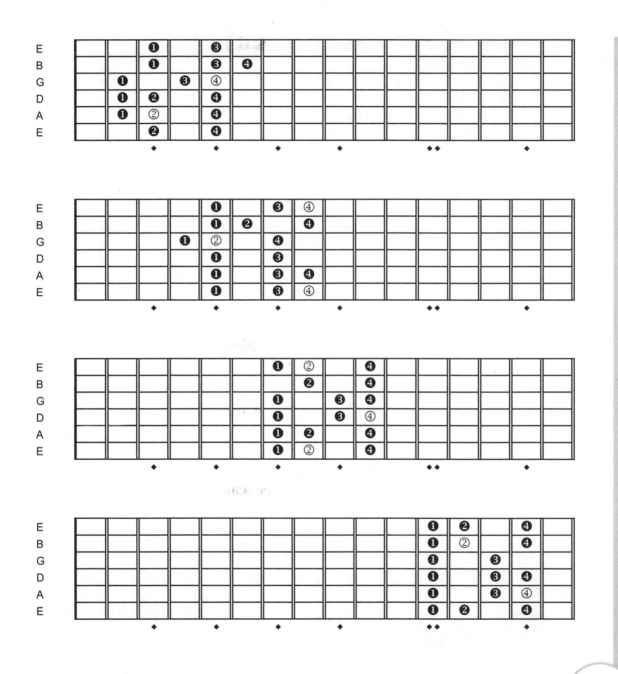

The Major/Ionian Scale

The Major/Ionian Scale

D Major

D♯/E♭ Major

The Major/Ionian Scale

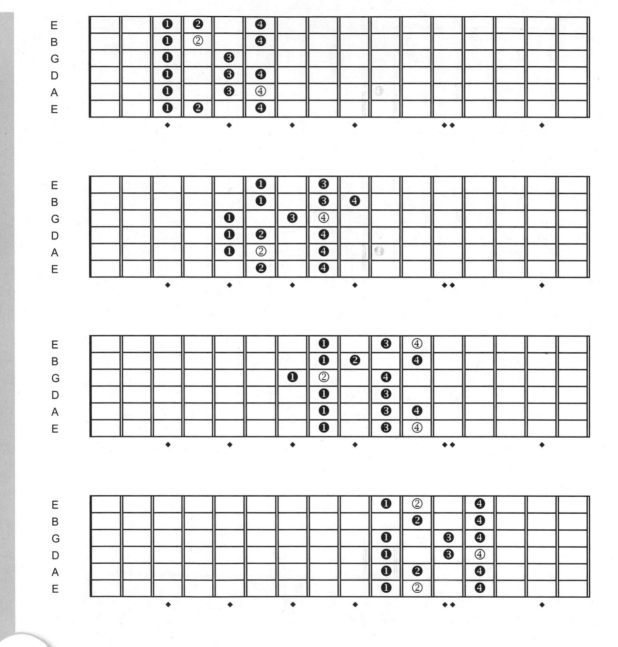

Track 3

E Major

The Major/Ionian Scale

F Major

The Major/Ionian Scale

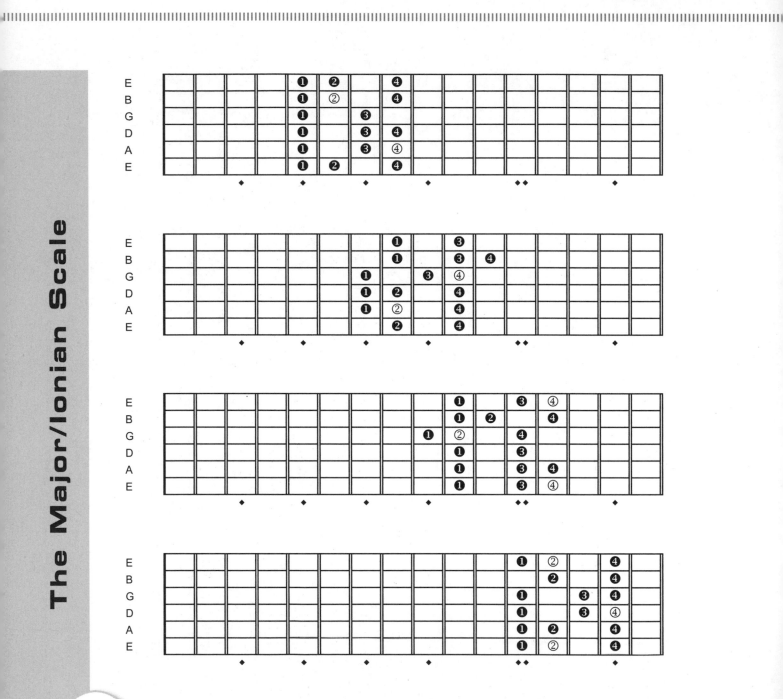

F#/G♭ Major

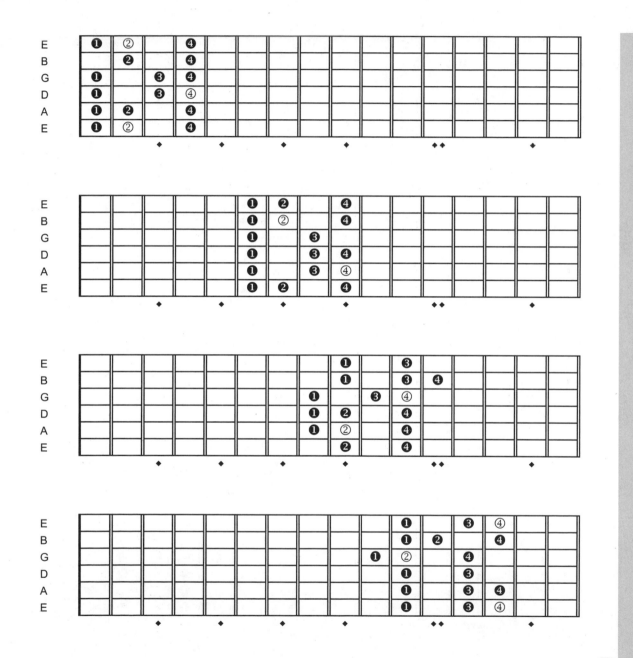

G Major

The Major/Ionian Scale

G#/Ab Major

A Major

The Major/Ionian Scale

A♯/B♭ Major

B Major

The Major/Ionian Scale

CHAPTER 3

The Minor Scale

The other staple of music theory is the minor scale/key, which is the other most commonly used scale and tonality in all of music. Minor scales encompass the darker, sadder sounds in music. You'll find minor scales in almost all styles of music, especially rock, jazz, and classical. No player's repertoire would be complete without some knowledge of the minor scale.

The Minor/Aeolian Scale in All Twelve Keys

If the major scale is the calming and happy scale, then the minor scale is its alter ego—darker and more melancholy. The minor scale in C would use the notes C, D, E♭, F, G, A♭, B♭, C, and its formula in scale degrees would be 1, 2, ♭3, 4, 5, ♭6, ♭7. You find the minor scale (yet again) in almost all styles of music, but you hear it in rock, hard rock, metal, Latin, jazz, and classical most often. You'd use it to improvise over minor chord progressions/keys. The minor scale is another vestige from the ancient church modes, and it goes by the alternate name "the Aeolian mode." Both names refer to the same scale.

C Minor

The Minor/Aeolian Scale

C#/Db Minor

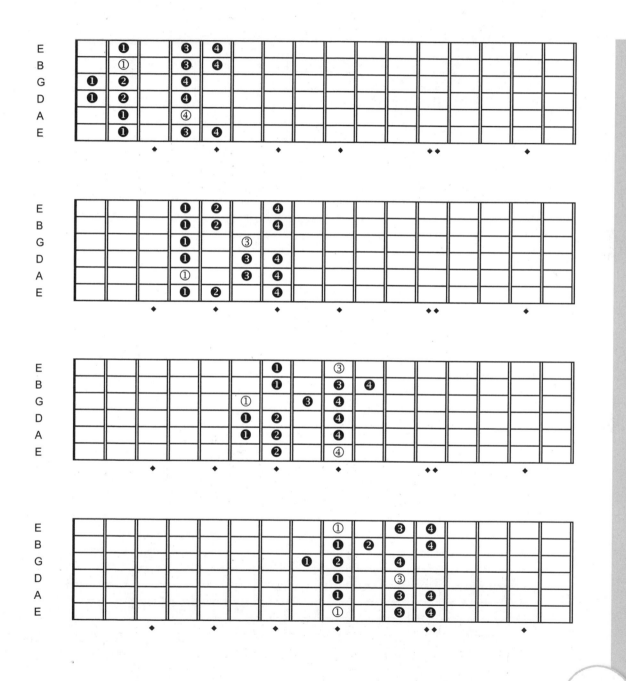

The Minor/Aeolian Scale

D Minor

The Minor/Aeolian Scale

D#/E♭ Minor

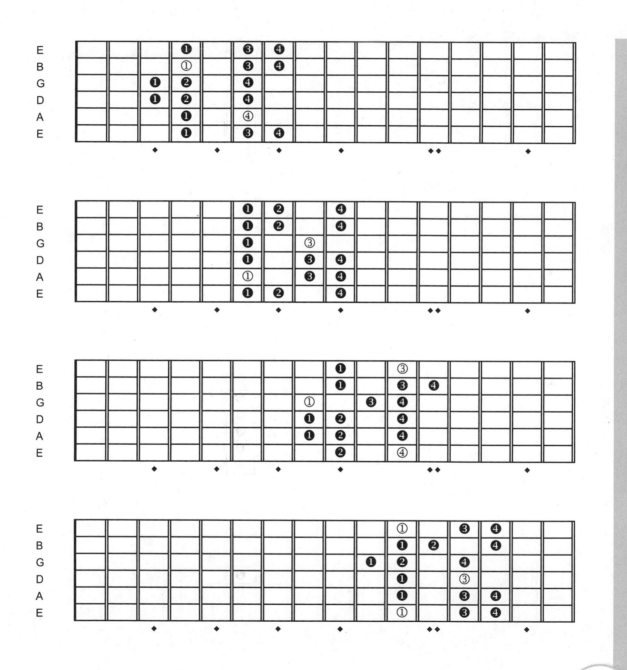

The Minor/Aeolian Scale

Track 4

E Minor

The Minor/Aeolian Scale

F Minor

F#/Gb Minor

The Minor/Aeolian Scale

G Minor

The Minor/Aeolian Scale

G#/A♭ Minor

The Minor/Aeolian Scale

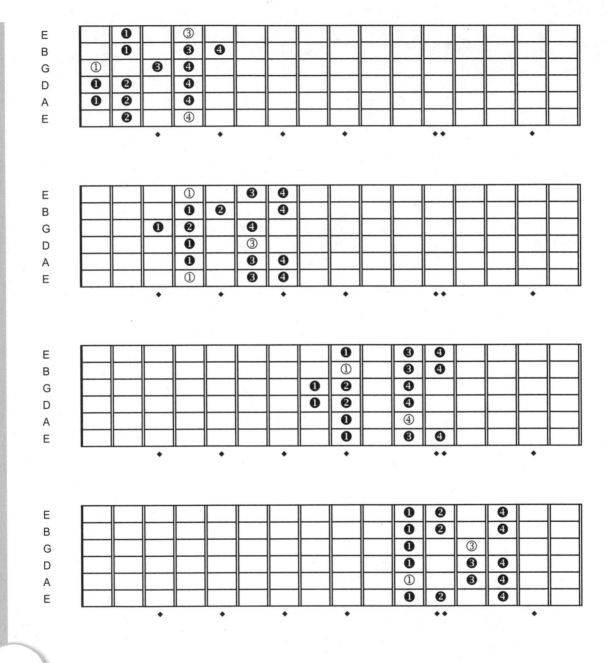

A Minor

The Minor/Aeolian Scale

A♯/B♭ Minor

The Minor/Aeolian Scale

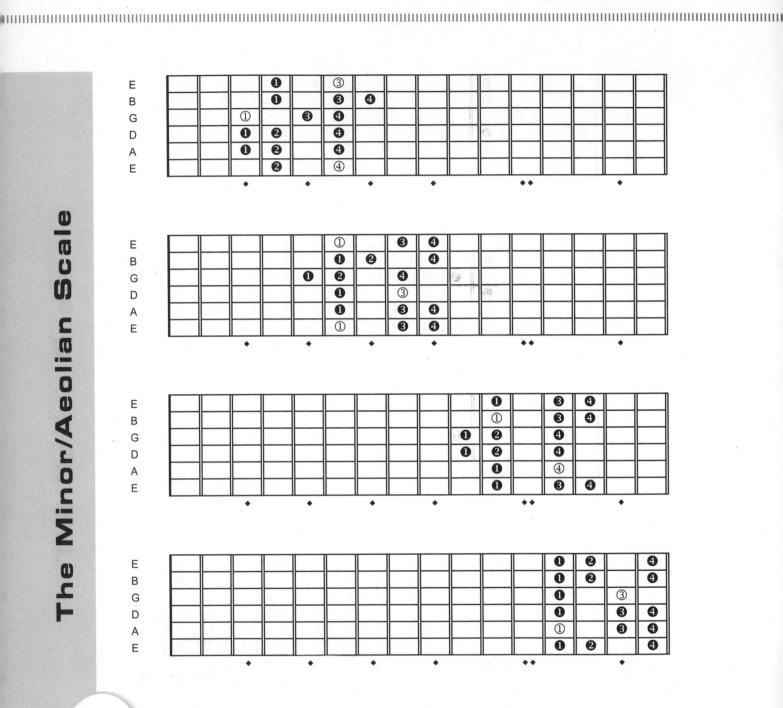

B Minor

CHAPTER 4

The Special Minor Scales

There are other types of minor scales than just the traditional minor/Aeolian scale. Throughout music history, two variant scales exist: harmonic and melodic minor. The variant scales came to light during analysis of classical music, but that hasn't stopped these scales from being utilized by jazz, rock, and ethnic musicians as well.

The Harmonic Minor Scale in All Twelve Keys

In classical music, the natural minor scale just wasn't working to make the right-sounding chords and progressions, so the composers started adapting the scales to make them sound a bit more harmonic. The result is the harmonic minor scale, which in C would have the notes C, D, E♭, F, G, A♭, B, C and the formula in scale degrees of 1, 2, ♭3, 4, 5, ♭6, 7. You hear this scale in many different ethnic cultures, in classical music as well as jazz, and in some heavy metal as well. It's the kind of scale that has a very unique sound, and most people find it "ethnic" sounding.

   Harmonic minor is one of the only scales than you can use to create melodies and improvise over a minor/major 7th chord.

The Melodic Minor Scale in All Twelve Keys

Composers used the harmonic minor scale to make the harmony of the minor key sound a bit better, but the result was a slightly odd melodic scale. To rectify this, the melodic minor scale was born; it is simply another adaptation of the natural minor scale. In C, the notes would be C, D, E♭, F, G, A, B, C, and the formula in scale degrees would be 1, 2, ♭3, 4, 5, 6, 7. The melodic minor scale is a very popular jazz scale. Though you get to hear it in rock from time to time, it's certainly a unique scale. It sounds like a half-major, half-minor scale.

   Melodic minor is the other scale that you can use to create melodies and improvise over a minor/major 7th chord.

C Harmonic Minor

The Harmonic Minor Scale

C#/D♭ Harmonic Minor

The Harmonic Minor Scale

D Harmonic Minor

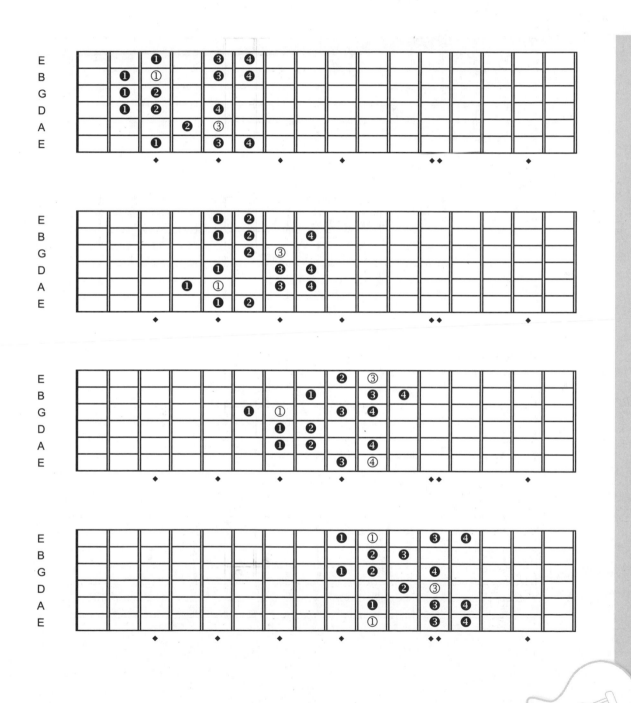

The Harmonic Minor Scale

D#/E♭ Harmonic Minor

The Harmonic Minor Scale

Track 5

E Harmonic Minor

F Harmonic Minor

The Harmonic Minor Scale

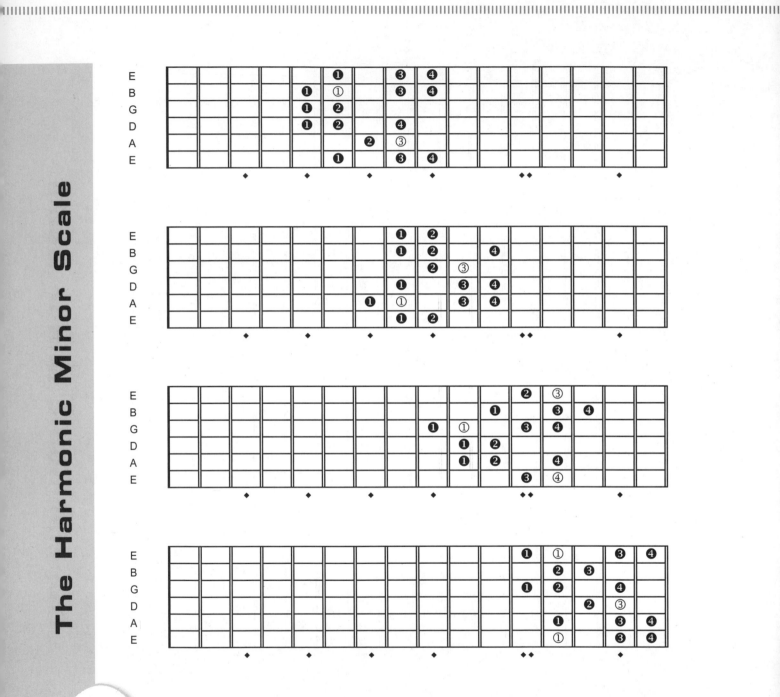

F♯/G♭ Harmonic Minor

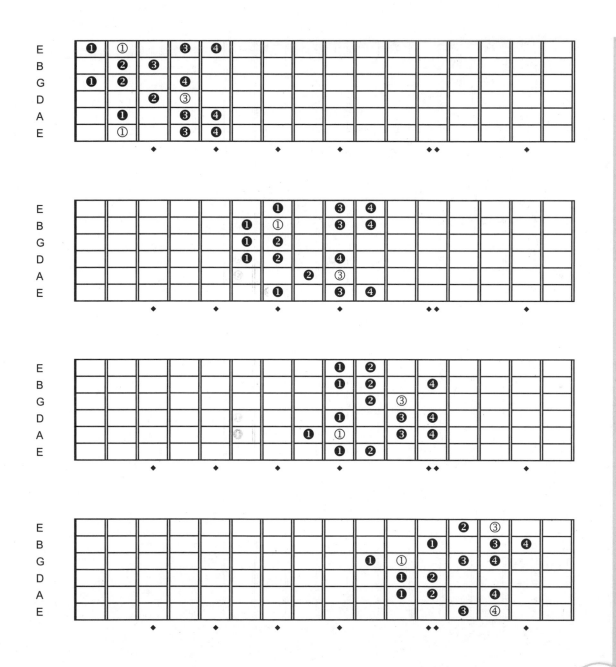

The Harmonic Minor Scale

G Harmonic Minor

The Harmonic Minor Scale

G♯/A♭ Harmonic Minor

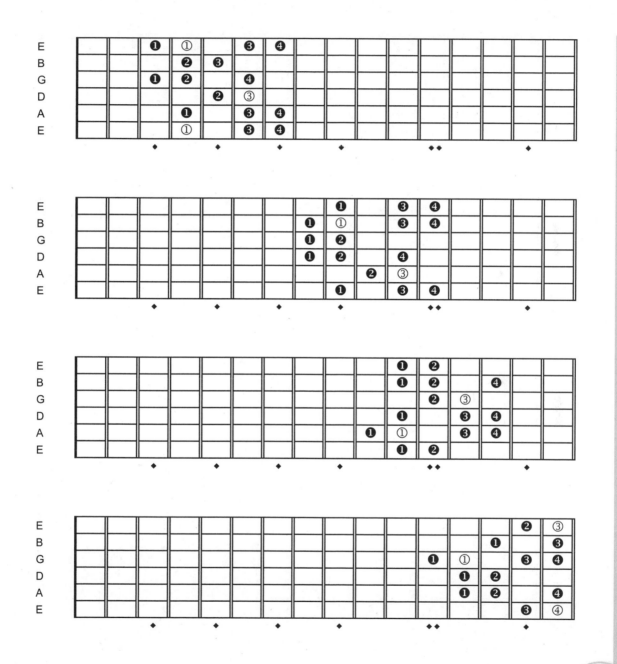

The Harmonic Minor Scale

A Harmonic Minor

The Harmonic Minor Scale

A♯/B♭ Harmonic Minor

The Harmonic Minor Scale

B Harmonic Minor

The Harmonic Minor Scale

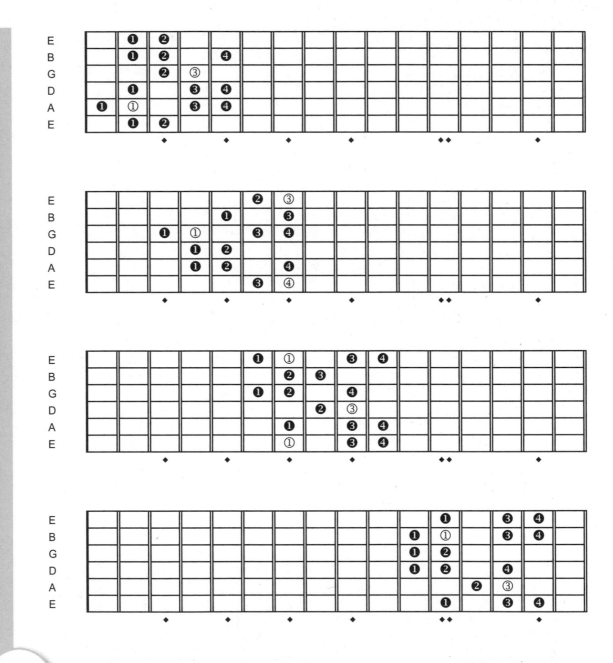

C Melodic Minor

C#/D♭ Melodic Minor

The Melodic Minor Scale

D Melodic Minor

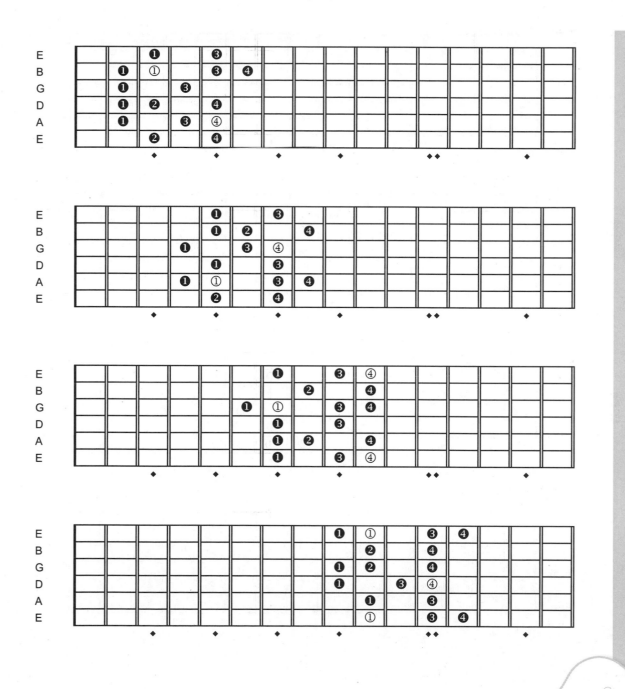

The Melodic Minor Scale

D♯/E♭ Melodic Minor

The Melodic Minor Scale

Track 6

E Melodic Minor

The Melodic Minor Scale

F Melodic Minor

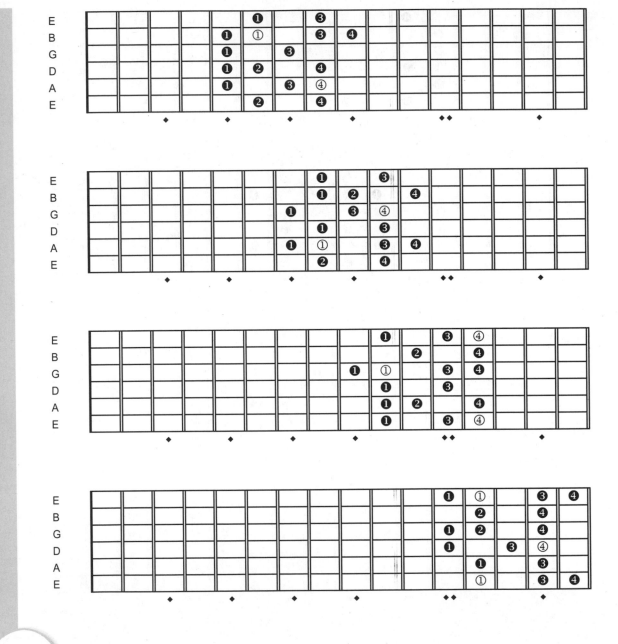

F#/G♭ Melodic Minor

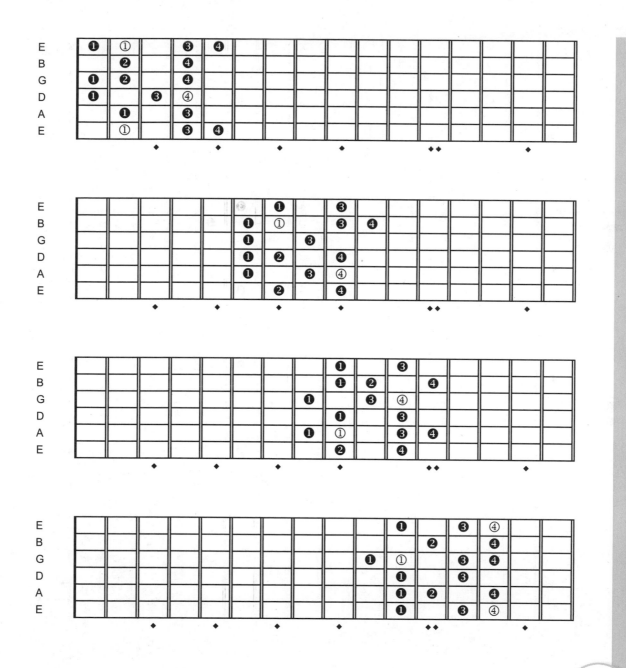

The Melodic Minor Scale

G Melodic Minor

The Melodic Minor Scale

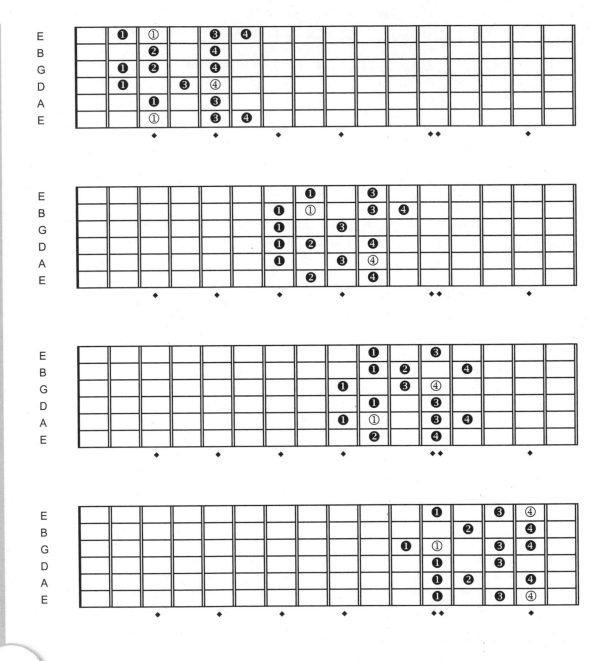

G#/A♭ Melodic Minor

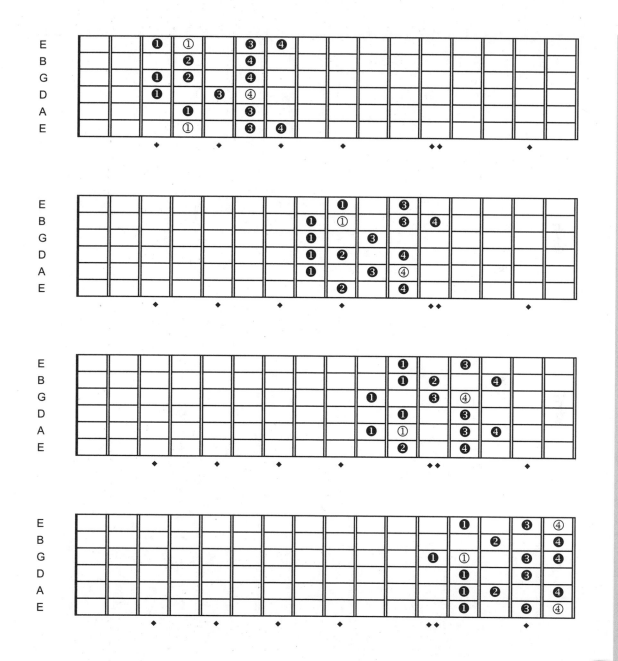

The Melodic Minor Scale

A Melodic Minor

The Melodic Minor Scale

A♯/B♭ Melodic Minor

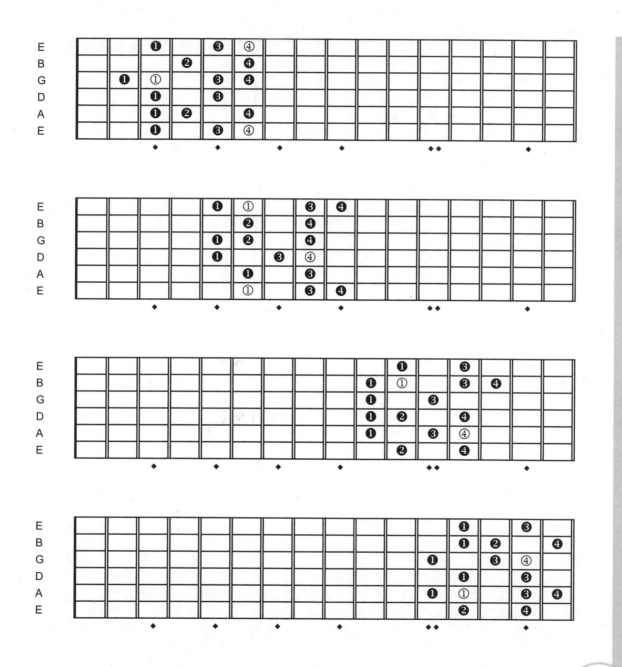

The Melodic Minor Scale

B Melodic Minor

The Melodic Minor Scale

CHAPTER 5

The Dorian Scale

Chapters 5 though 9 are devoted to the rest of the church modes, an ancient set of scales that were used widely in Gregorian chants and other sacred music. The Dorian scale is one of the modes that has not only survived but flourished. You find the Dorian mode used extensively in jazz, for example.

The Dorian Scale in All Twelve Keys

The Dorian scale (or mode) is actually a very interesting scale. It's based on the major scale, but it's displaced (meaning you start from a note other than the root). Dorian is the 2nd mode of the major scale. This information won't change how you play it, but it will give you some good information to use at parties! The Dorian scale from C would spell as C, D, E♭, F, G, A, B♭, C, and its formula in scale degrees would be 1, 2, ♭3, 4, 5, 6, ♭7.

You find the Dorian scale most often in blues and jazz, but it's equally at home in rock. If you're looking to supercharge your minor pentatonic scale, try Dorian from the same root instead. Typically, most musicians play the Dorian scale when they are trying to create melodies or improvise over minor chords. Also, since the spelling of the Dorian scale is very close to that of a traditional minor scale, you may use the Dorian scale as a variation when you want to sound minor but need something a little different. In jazz, Dorian is the de facto minor scale.

C Dorian

The Dorian Scale

C#/D♭ Dorian

D Dorian

The Dorian Scale

D#/E♭ Dorian

Track 7

E Dorian

The Dorian Scale

F Dorian

F#/G♭ Dorian

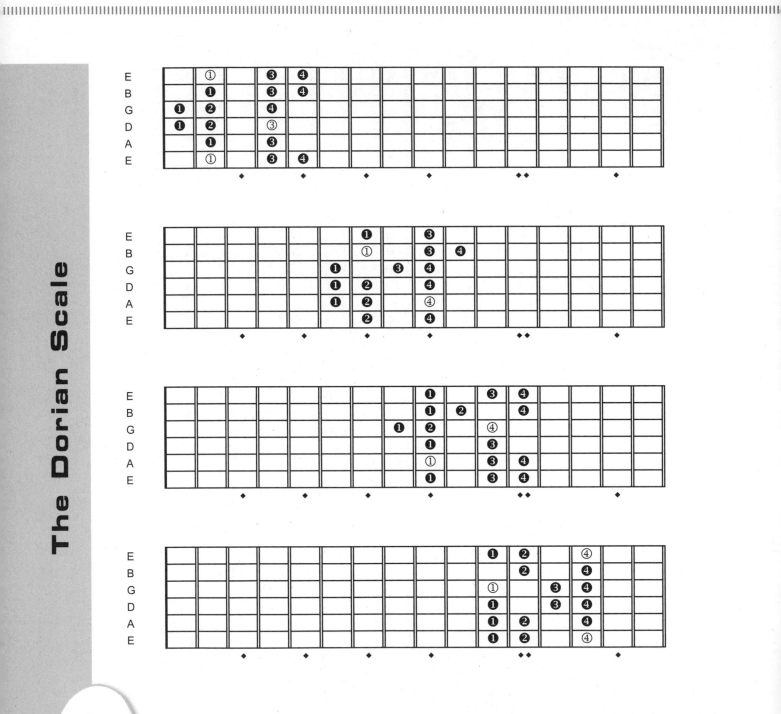

The Dorian Scale

G Dorian

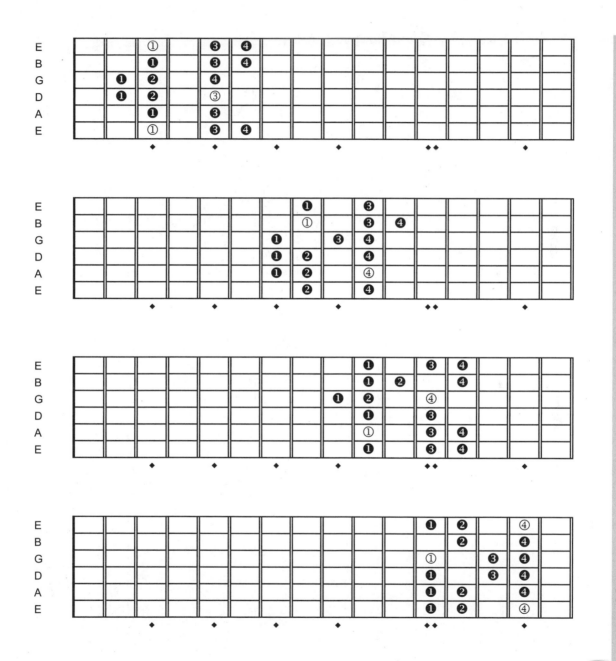

G#/A♭ Dorian

The Dorian Scale

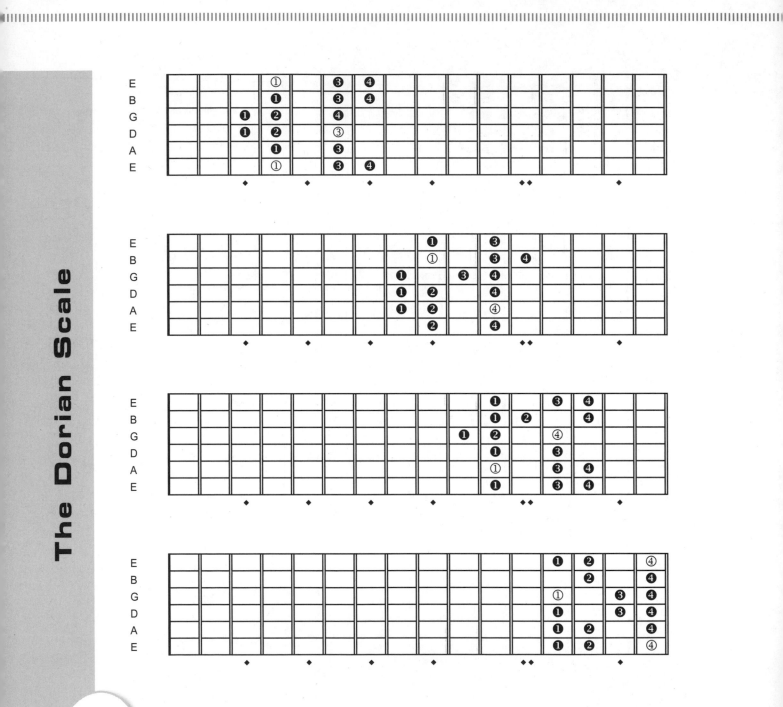

A Dorian

A#/B♭ Dorian

The Dorian Scale

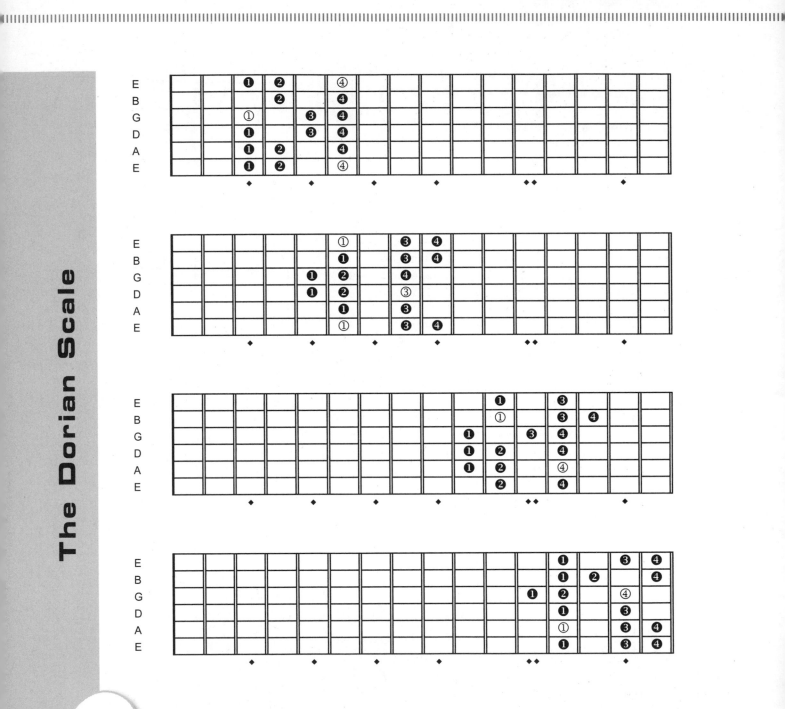

B Dorian

The Dorian Scale

CHAPTER 6

The Phrygian Scale

The Phrygian scale is one of the church modes that you still hear from time to time. This very 'Spanish' mode is used not only in the music of Spain but also in rock and jazz music. It has a dark, spiritual quality that many musicians enjoy.

The Phrygian Scale in All Twelve Keys

The Phrygian scale is another church mode. It is derived from a single major scale, just displaced. (Phrygian is the 3rd mode of the major scale.) The Phrygian is definitely not a scale you hear every day, but it's nonetheless a beautiful scale, very popular in the national music of Spain and, oddly enough, in heavy metal. In C, the scale spells as C, D♭, E♭, F, G, A♭, B♭, and its formula in scale degrees is 1, ♭2, ♭3, 4, 5, ♭6, ♭7. You can use this scale over a single minor chord (say in a vamp) or to compose a melody with a Spanish feel. It's a pretty but dark-sounding scale. The scale is easily identified by its characteristic half step between the root and the second pitch.

C Phrygian

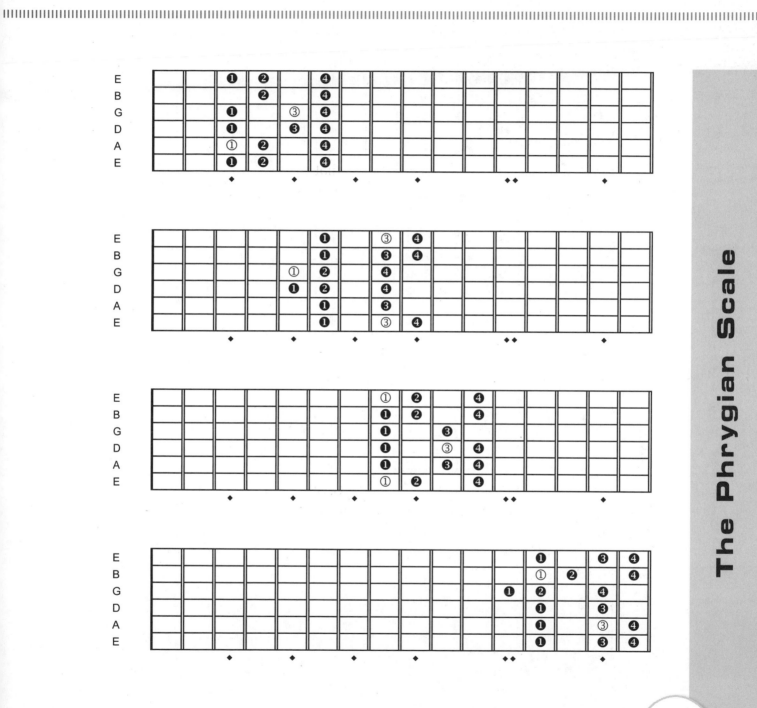

The Phrygian Scale

D Phrygian

D#/E♭ Phrygian

The Phrygian Scale

Track 8

E Phrygian

The Phrygian Scale

F Phrygian

The Phrygian Scale

F♯/G♭ Phrygian

G Phrygian

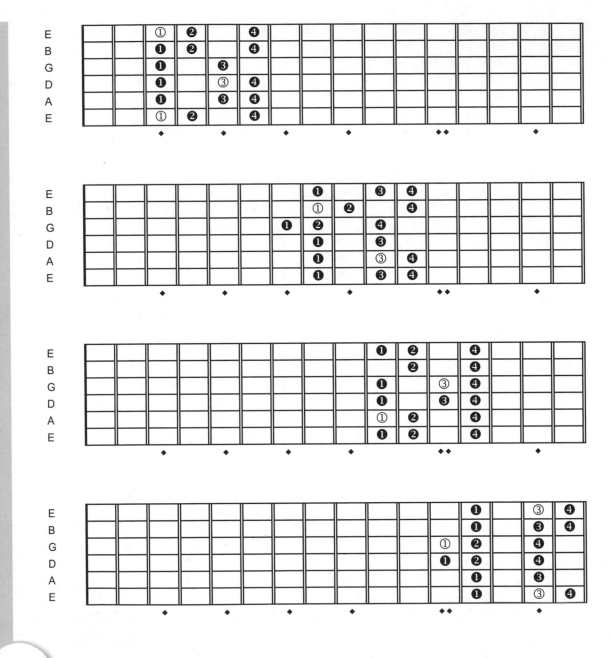

The Phrygian Scale

G#/A♭ Phrygian

A Phrygian

The Phrygian Scale

A#/B♭ Phrygian

The Phrygian Scale

B Phrygian

The Phrygian Scale

CHAPTER 7

The Lydian Scale

The Lydian scale is a beautiful, haunting scale that has survived a long time. The Lydian mode is often used as a replacement to the major scale because of its alteration to the 4th tone. Many rock and jazz musicians use the Lydian mode for improvisation and for creating melodies.

The Lydian Scale in All Twelve Keys

The Lydian scale is one of the most unusual scales derived from the ancient church modes. Another church mode, the Lydian scale is derived from a single major scale, just displaced. (Lydian is the 4th mode of the major scale.) It has a bright, airy sound that many composers and musicians favor. You hear this scale all the time in film scores, as its majestic sound is easily conveyed to equally majestic scenes. In C, the scale spells as C, D, E, F♯, G, A, B, C, and its formula in scale degrees is 1, 2, 3, ♯4, 5, 6, 7. The Lydian scale sounds like a major-type scale, but the raised 4th note gives it its unique sound. You hear Lydian used in rock, jazz, classical, and film scores mostly, although it's been known to pop up anywhere.

The Lydian scale is one of the only scales that you can play when creating melodies or improvising over a major 7♯11 chord.

C Lydian

The Lydian Scale

C#/D♭ Lydian

D Lydian

The Lydian Scale

D♯/E♭ Lydian

Track 9

E Lydian

The Lydian Scale

F Lydian

F#/G♭ Lydian

The Lydian Scale

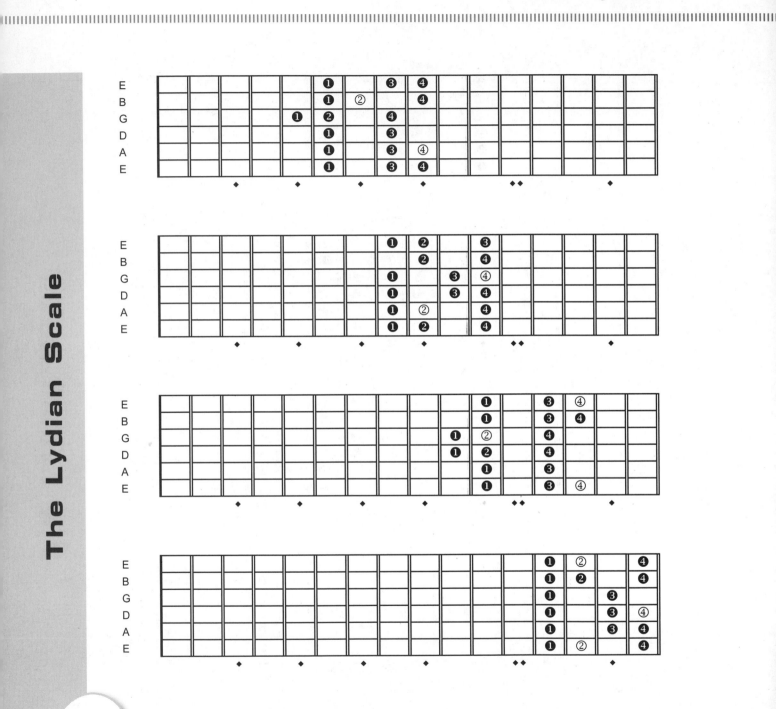

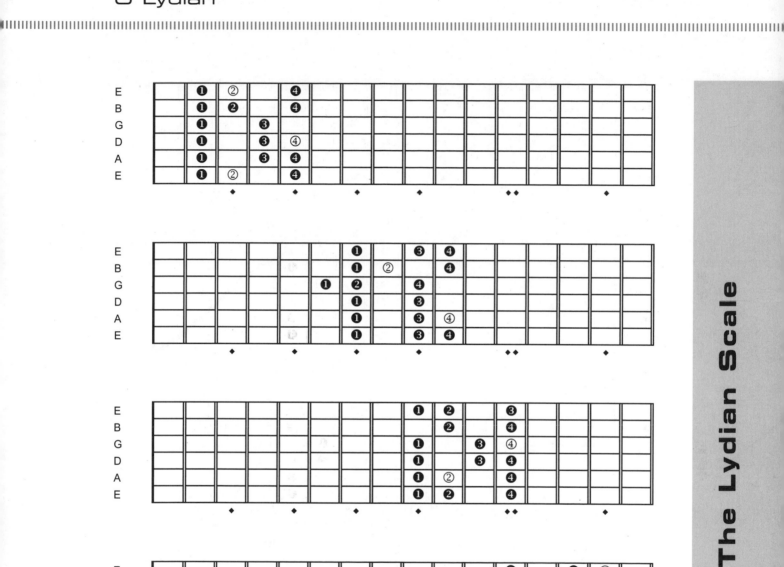

G Lydian

The Lydian Scale

G#/A♭ Lydian

The Lydian Scale

A Lydian

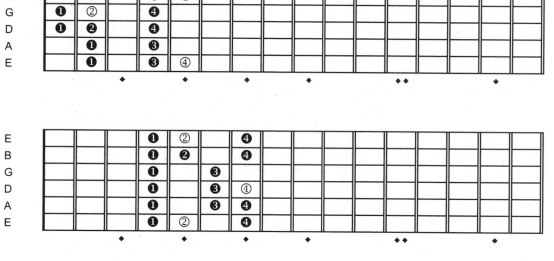

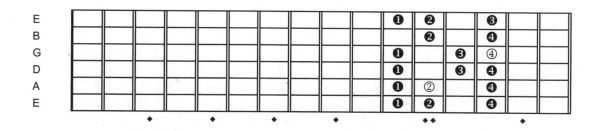

The Lydian Scale

A♯/B♭ Lydian

The Lydian Scale

B Lydian

The Lydian Scale

CHAPTER 8

The Mixolydian Scale

The Mixolydian is an extremely popular scale that has seen adoption in rock and blues music. The Mixolydian mode is a darker, blusier major scale that highlights the dominant, or "flat," seventh scale degree. Not just for jazz and blues musicians, this mode is a staple of Celtic and other traditional northern European music.

The Mixolydian Scale in All Twelve Keys

The Mixolydian scale is another really old scale that refuses to go away. Another church mode, the Mixolydian scale is derived from a single major scale, just displaced. (Mixolydian is the 5th mode of the major scale.) In C, the scale spells as C, D, E, F, G, A, B♭, C, and its formula in scale degrees is 1, 2, 3, 4, 5, 6, ♭7.

The Mixolydian scale sounds like a bluesy major scale and is used in rock, blues, jazz, and jam band music. It's a favorite scale of Jerry Garcia and others in the jam band movement. It's a perfect blues scale, ripe with possibilities and beautiful melodic tools. In addition to its bluesy vibe, it's one of the best scales you can play over the equally bluesy dominant seventh chord (such as C7).

C Mixolydian

C#/Db Mixolydian

The Mixolydian Scale

D Mixolydian

D#/E♭ Mixolydian

The Mixolydian Scale

Track 10

E Mixolydian

The Mixolydian Scale

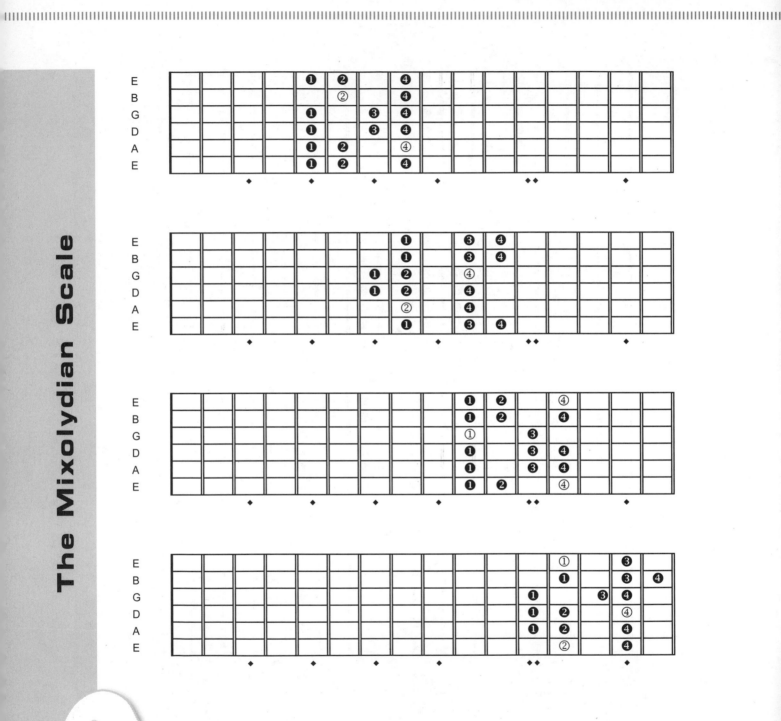

F Mixolydian

The Mixolydian Scale

F#/G♭ Mixolydian

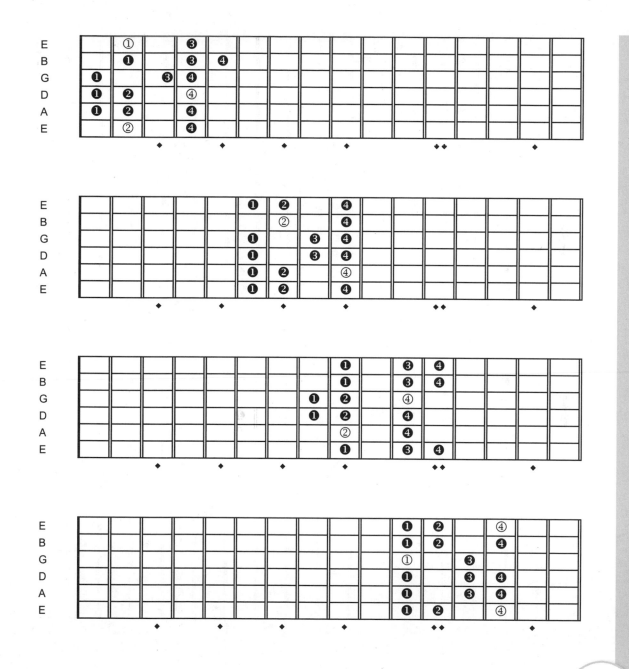

G Mixolydian

The Mixolydian Scale

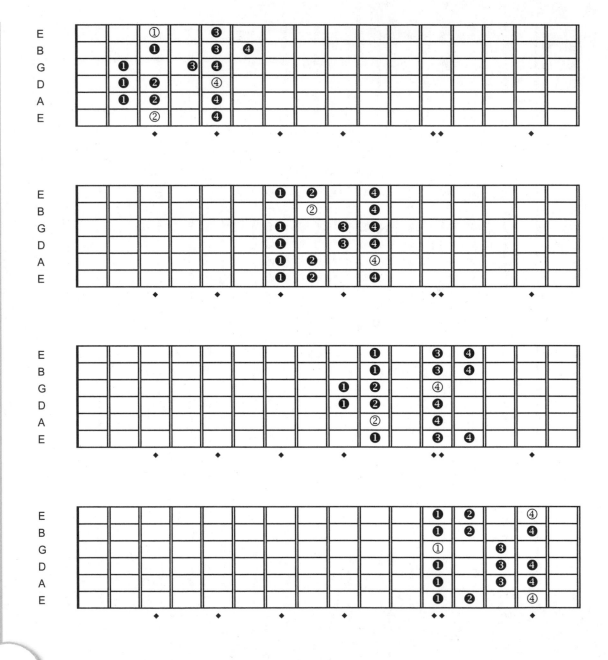

G#/A♭ Mixolydian

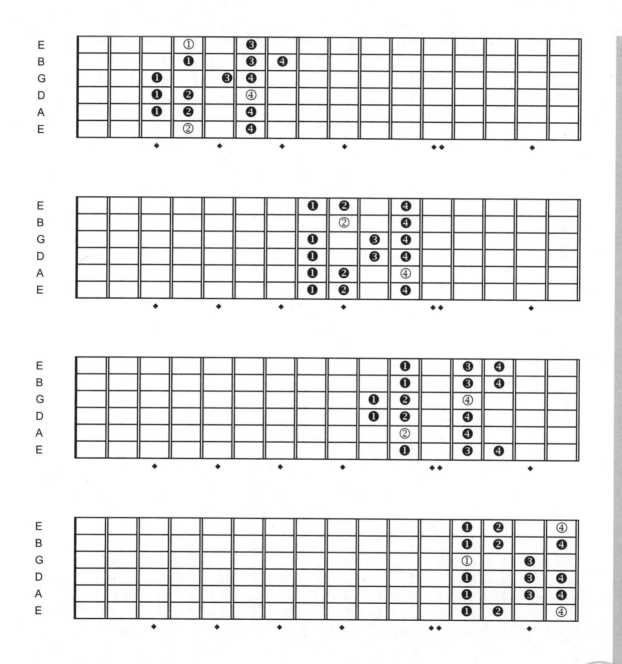

The Mixolydian Scale

A Mixolydian

The Mixolydian Scale

A#/B♭ Mixolydian

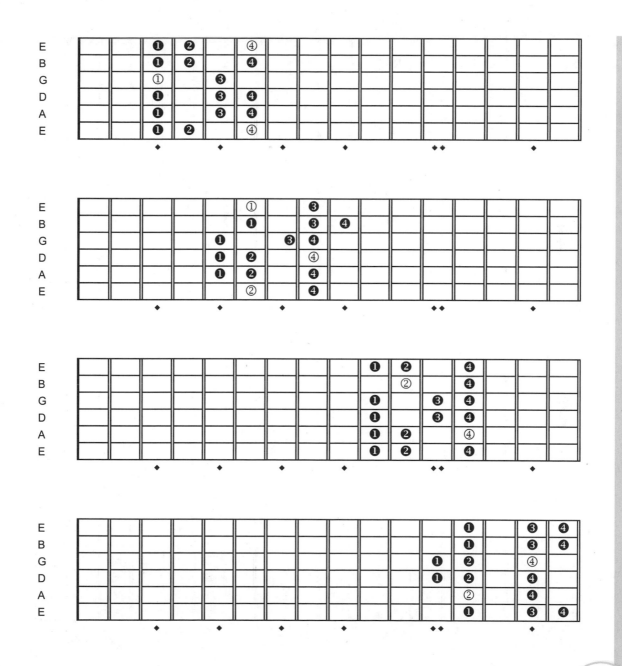

The Mixolydian Scale

B Mixolydian

The Mixolydian Scale

The Locrian Scale

Chapter 9 is devoted to the Locrian Scale, the last of the church modes, an ancient set of scales that were used widely in Gregorian chants and other sacred music. The Locrian scale is unfortunately just not that popular. The combination of ♭2 and ♭5 make Locrian a very unusual scale indeed. Nevertheless, musicians still find ways to use this scale, especially when used over a minor 7♭five chord (half-diminished).

The Locrian Scale in All Twelve Keys

The Locrian scale is the last mode (that is, the 7th mode of the major scale) and is a rather odd sound. It's very dark, with tinges of minor, with a very dissonant quality. From C, the notes are C, D♭, E♭, F, G♭, A♭, B♭, and its formula in scale degrees is 1, ♭2, ♭3, 4, ♭5, ♭6, ♭7. The Locrian hasn't been totally abandoned; Metallica used in it in their song "Wherever I May Roam."

The Locrian scale is important because it's one of the scales you can play over the minor 7♭5/half-diminished chord. Additionally, if you're going to study the church modes, you might as well learn them all.

C Locrian

The Locrian Scale

C#/D♭ Locrian

D Locrian

The Locrian Scale

D#/E♭ Locrian

Track 11

E Locrian

The Locrian Scale

F Locrian

F♯/G♭ Locrian

The Locrian Scale

G Locrian

G#/Ab Locrian

The Locrian Scale

A Locrian

A#/B♭ Locrian

The Locrian Scale

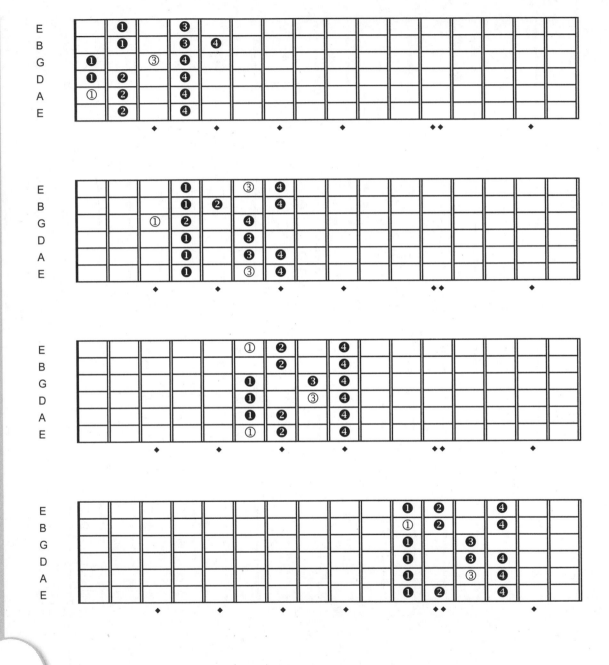

B Locrian

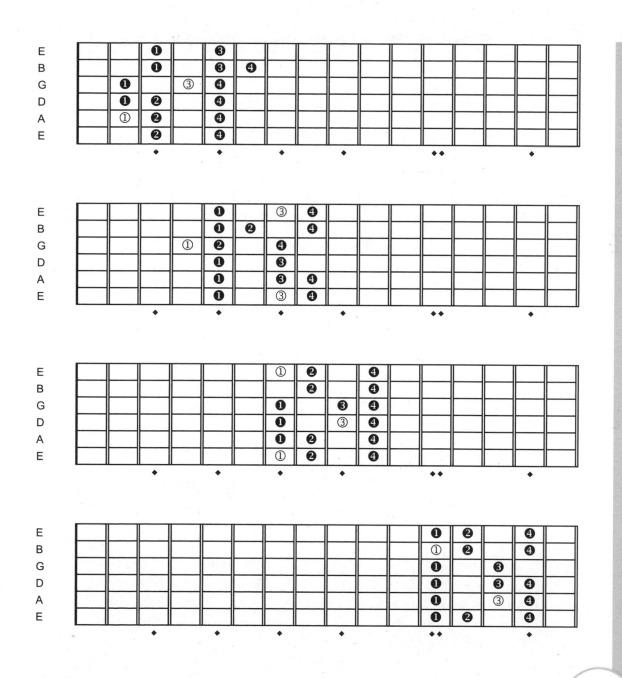

The Locrian Scale

CHAPTER 10

The Whole-Tone Scale

The whole-tone scale is your first look at a scale that is purely mathematical, based on a set of repeating intervals. In this case, the intervals are whole steps, or whole tones. This scale is used in classical, jazz, and rock music and also finds its way into film scores. You'll hear whole-tone scales in the soundtrack for Looney Tunes cartoons. The next time you see a character sleeping and dreaming, you'll likely hear the whole-tone scale.

The Whole-Tone Scale in All Twelve Keys

The whole-tone scale is considered a symmetrical scale because it's comprised entirely of whole steps (or whole tones). It's also a six-note scale (which is rare, because almost every other scale in the book is a seven-note scale). What's even cooler is that there are only two whole-tone scales, one starting on C, and the other starting on C#/D♭. Start anywhere else, and you'll get the same notes! Even when you look at the scale charts, the patterns look symmetric, as they repeat across the neck. From C, the whole-tone scale spells as C, D, E, F#, G#, A# or as a formula based on intervals as 1, 2, 3, #4, #5, #6. It's a neat sounding scale, and it definitely has its uses.

In addition to the musicians who composed those dream sequence scores for the Looney Tunes cartoons, classical composer Maurice Ravel was a big fan of this scale, as were many of the impressionist composers. Frank Zappa was also very fond of this scale. It's a really interesting sound that you should try, and it's also easy to play on the neck.

The whole-tone scale is one of the best, and only, scales to play over an augmented chord and the augmented 7th chord (such as C7+/C7#5).

C Whole-Tone

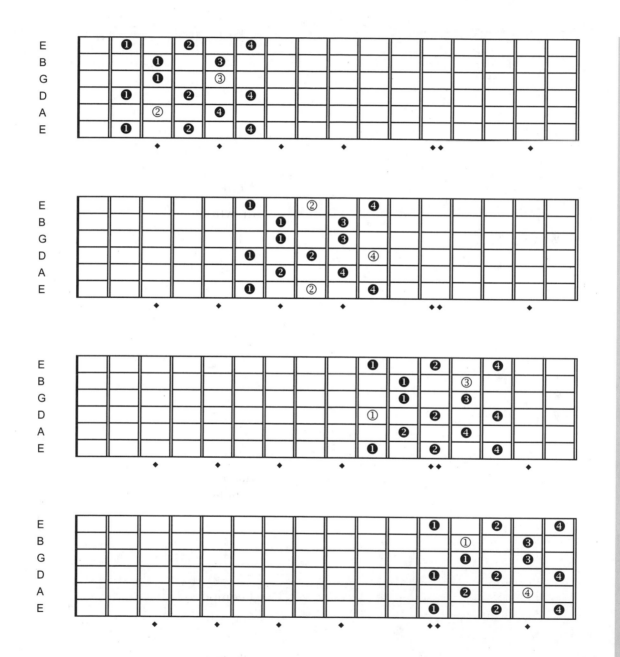

The Whole-Tone Scale

C#/D♭ Whole-Tone

The Whole-Tone Scale

D Whole-Tone

D#/E♭ Whole-Tone

The Whole-Tone Scale

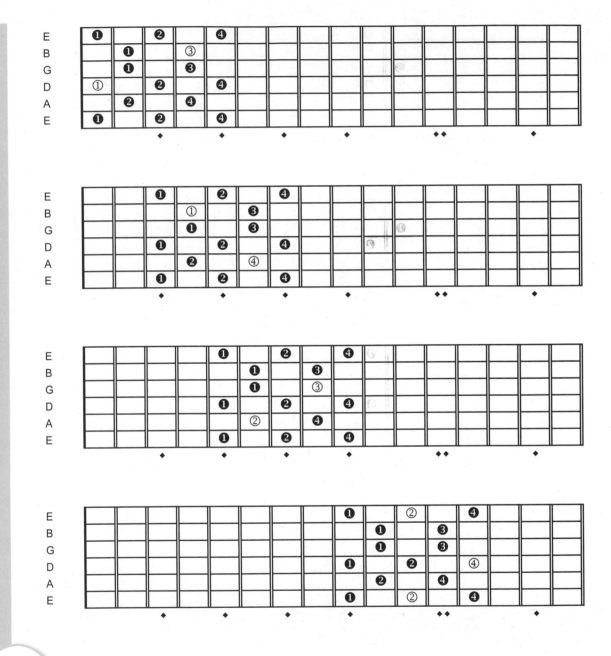

Track 12

E Whole-Tone

The Whole-Tone Scale

F Whole-Tone

The Whole-Tone Scale

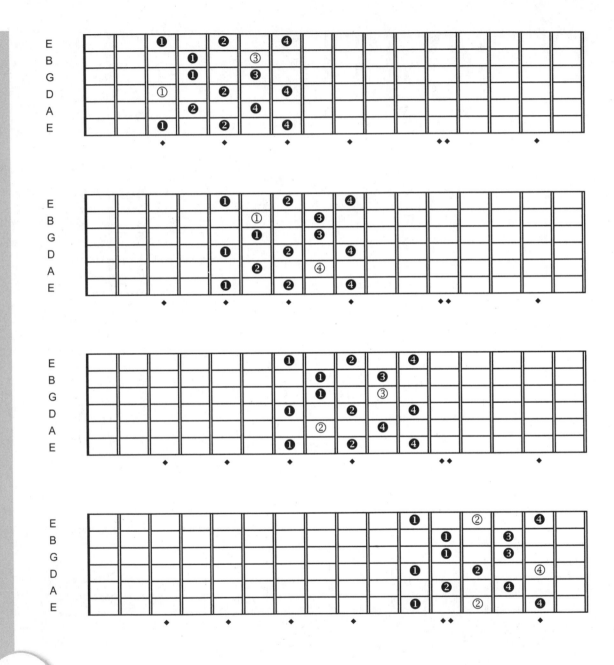

F♯/G♭ Whole-Tone

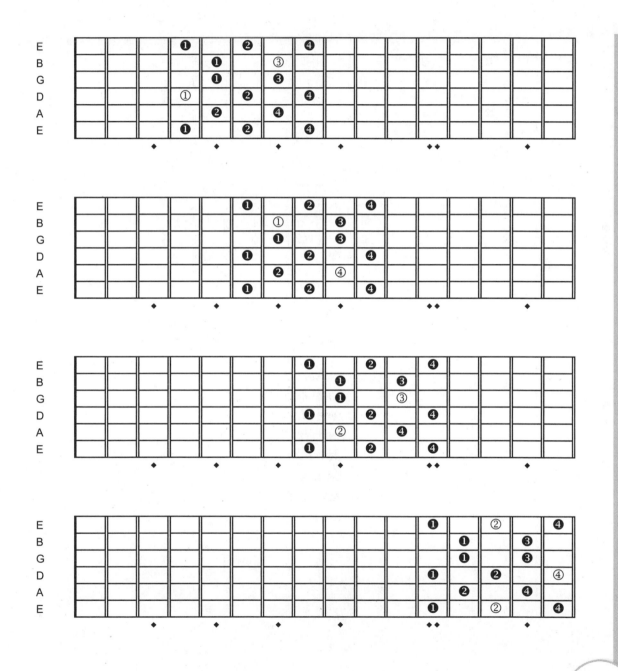

G Whole-Tone

The Whole-Tone Scale

G#/A♭ Whole-Tone

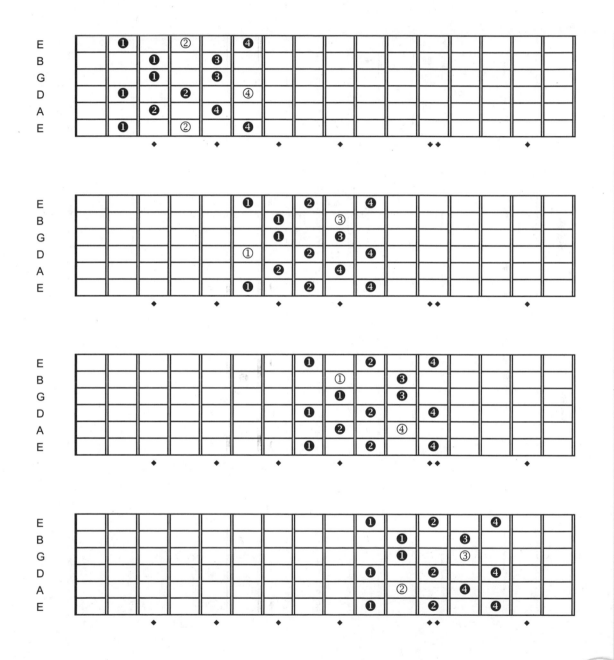

The Whole-Tone Scale

A Whole-Tone

The Whole-Tone Scale

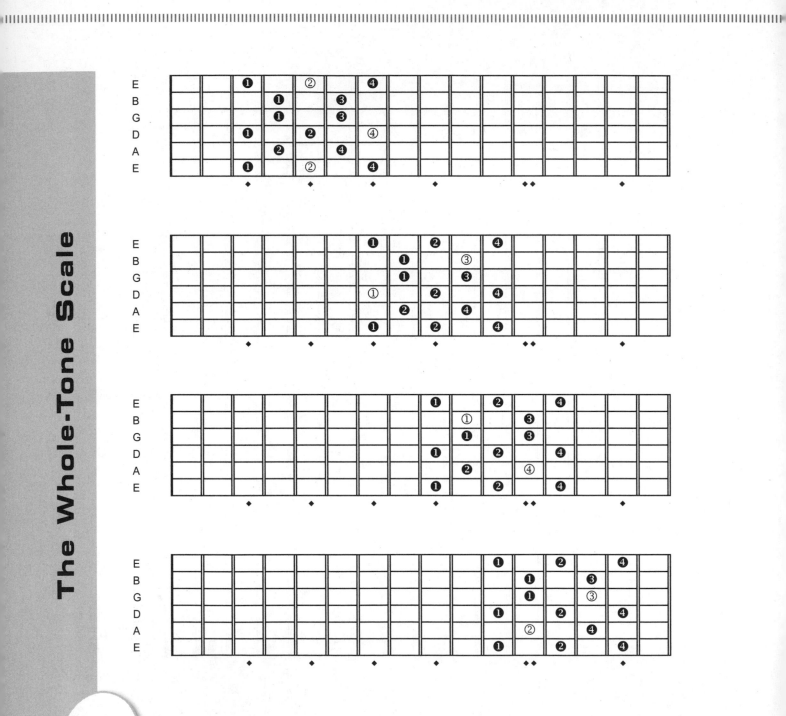

A♯/B♭ Whole-Tone

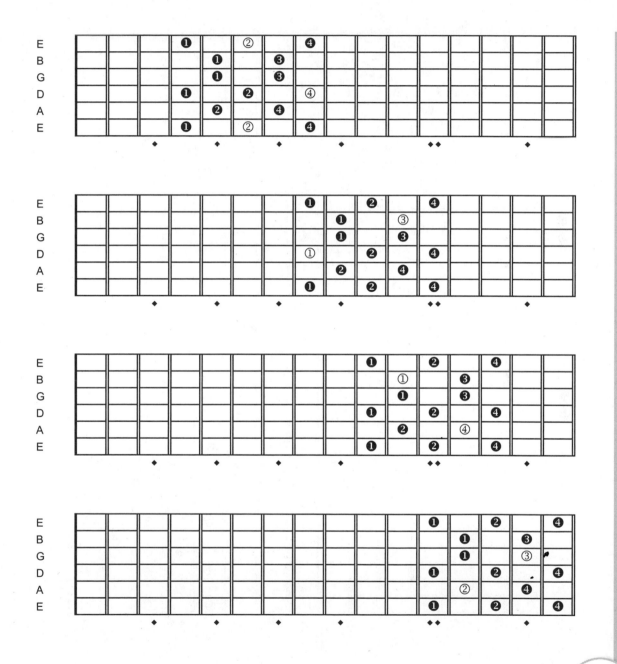

B Whole-Tone

The Whole-Tone Scale

CHAPTER 11

The Diminished Scales

Another set of symmetrical scales consists of the diminished or octatonic scales. These scales are based on repeating patterns of whole and half steps. There are two diminished scales in this book, named for the direction of their interval patterns. Diminished scales are also unique in that they're the only eight-note scales in this book. They are also unique in that these scales contain a symmetrical visual fingering on the guitar and are very easy to memorize.

The Half-Whole Diminished Scale in All Twelve Keys

The first diminished scale is the half-whole diminished scale, which is based on a symmetrical pattern of half and whole steps. You start from C, and progress a half step, then a whole step, and keep going until you get back to C, which is where you started. In C, this half whole diminished scale spells as C, D♭, E♭, E, F♯, G, A, B♭, C. Its formula in scale degrees is 1, ♭2/♭9, ♭3/♯9, 4, ♯4/♯11, 5, 6, ♭7.

This scale is primarily used by jazz musicians to solo over heavily altered 7th chords with natural 13ths (for instance, C13♯9). Yeah, it's an odd chord, but when it comes up, you'll have something to play. It's also used to create melodies and improvise over a diminished seventh chord (such as C dim7).

The Whole-Half Diminished Scale in All Twelve Keys

The other diminished scale is the whole-half diminished scale, which is based on a symmetrical pattern of whole and half steps. You start from C, and progress a whole step, then a half step, and keep going until you get back to C, which is where you started. In C, this whole half diminished scale spells as C, D, E♭, F, G♭, A♭, A, B, C, and its formula in scale degrees is 1, 2/9, ♭3/♯9, 4, ♭5, ♭6/♭13, 6/13, 7.

This particular diminished scale is primarily used to create melodies and improvise on a diminished 7th chord (e.g. C dim 7) or the much less seen C diminished/major 7 chord (C dim (maj7).

C Half-Whole Diminished

The Half-Whole Diminished Scale

C♯/D♭ Half-Whole Diminished

The Half-Whole Diminished Scale

D Half-Whole Diminished

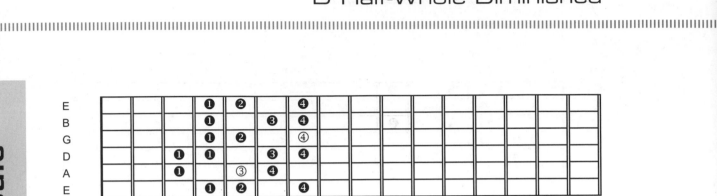

The Half-Whole Diminished Scale

D#/E♭ Half-Whole Diminished

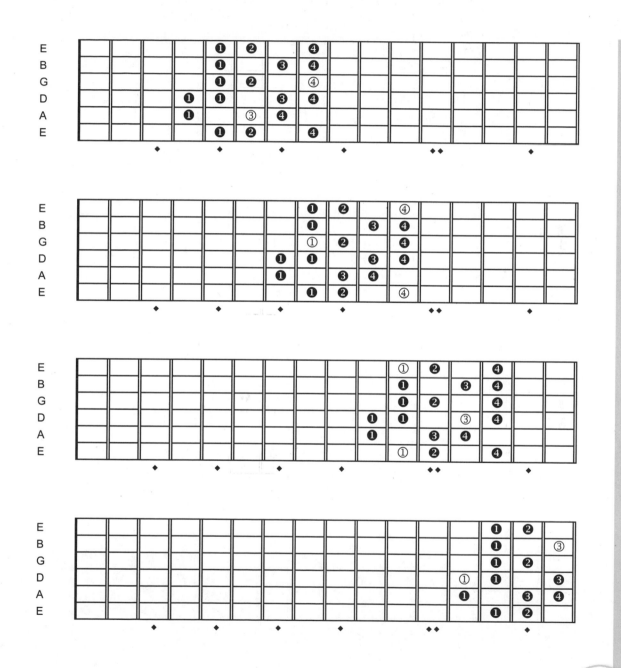

The Half-Whole Diminished Scale

Track 13

E Half-Whole Diminished

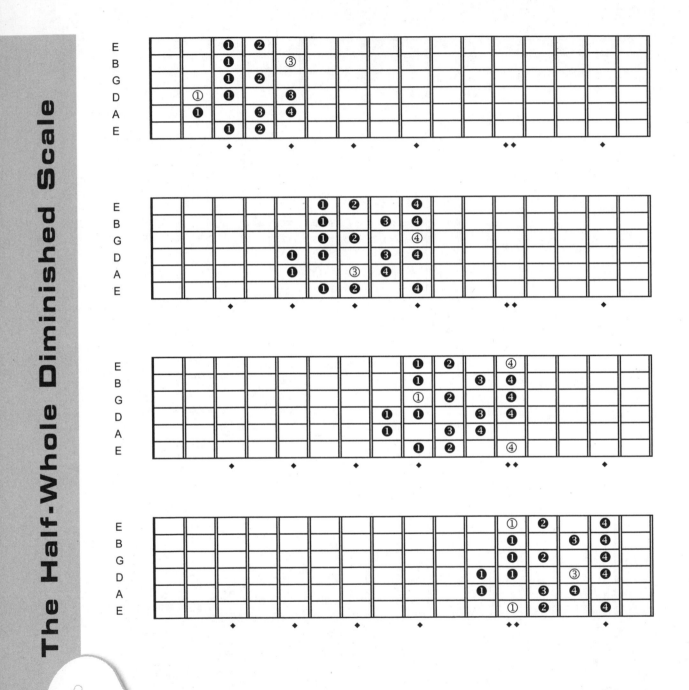

The Half-Whole Diminished Scale

F Half-Whole Diminished

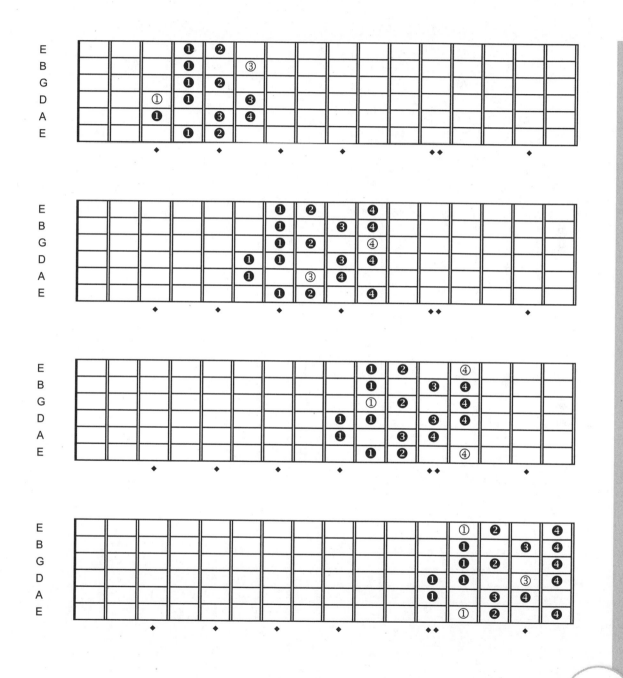

The Half-Whole Diminished Scale

F#/G♭ Half-Whole Diminished

The Half-Whole Diminished Scale

G Half-Whole Diminished

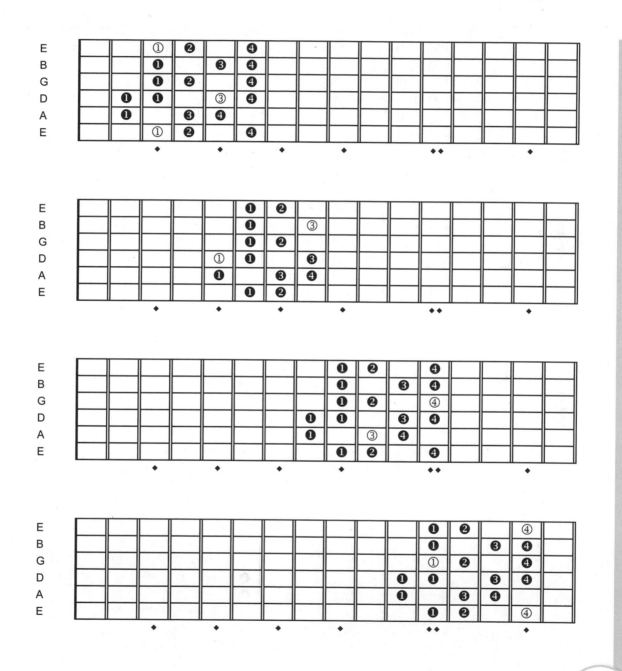

The Half-Whole Diminished Scale

G#/Ab Half-Whole Diminished

The Half-Whole Diminished Scale

A Half-Whole Diminished

A#/B♭ Half-Whole Diminished

The Half-Whole Diminished Scale

B Half-Whole Diminished

C Whole-Half Diminished

The Whole-Half Diminished Scale

C#/D♭ Whole-Half Diminished

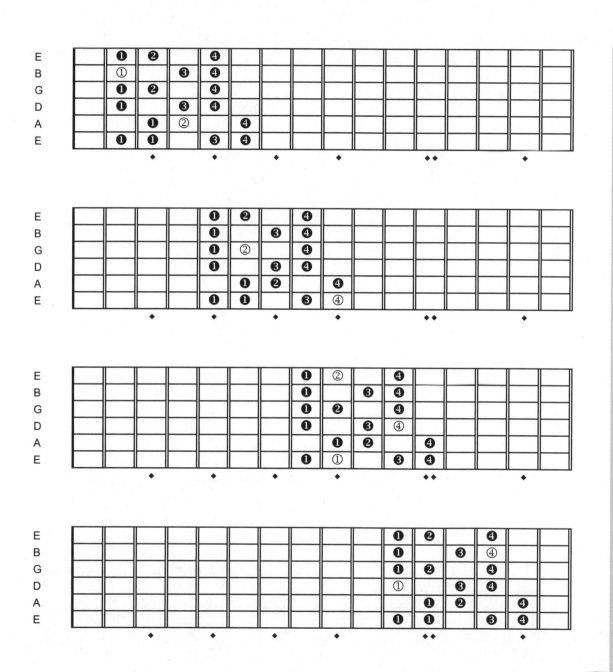

The Whole-Half Diminished Scale

D Whole-Half Diminished

The Whole-Half Diminished Scale

D♯/E♭ Whole-Half Diminished

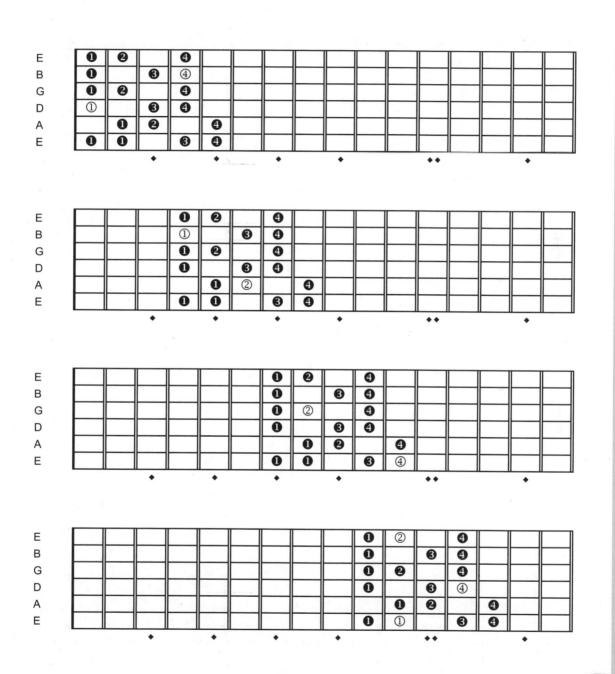

The Whole-Half Diminished Scale

Track 14

E Whole-Half Diminished

The Whole-Half Diminished Scale

F Whole-Half Diminished

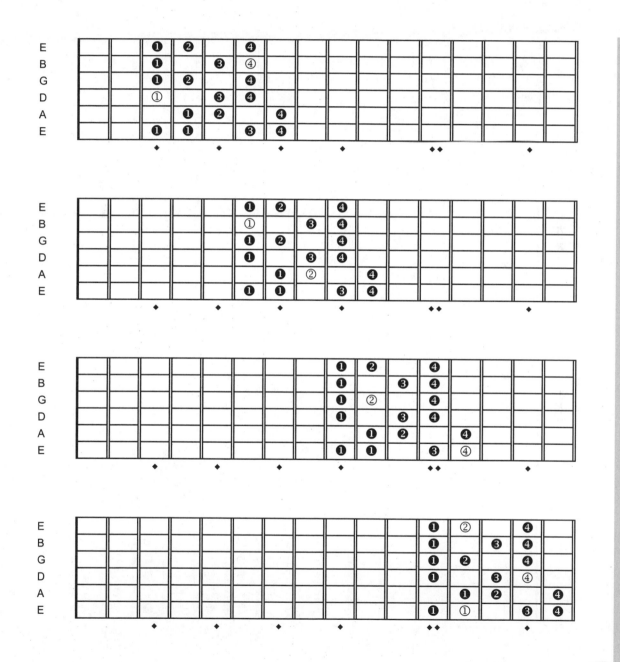

The Whole-Half Diminished Scale

F♯/G♭ Whole-Half Diminished

The Whole-Half Diminished Scale

G Whole-Half Diminished

G#/A♭ Whole-Half Diminished

The Whole-Half Diminished Scale

A Whole-Half Diminished

The Whole-Half Diminished Scale

A♯/B♭ Whole-Half Diminished

B Whole-Half Diminished

CHAPTER 12

Jazz/Modern Scales

The last chapter of this book deals with some unusual scales that are used mostly in jazz improvisation. The five scales in this chapter help take care of jazz music's occasional "difficult" chords. They also provide some of the sounds that make jazz what it is! If you're looking to take your playing into the modern era, take a look at these new scales!

The Bebop Dominant Scale in All Twelve Keys

The bebop dominant scale probably really isn't a scale in the traditional sense, but if you look at (or better yet, transcribe) jazz solos from the bebop era (such as those of Charlie Parker and Dizzy Gillespie), you'll see this configuration of notes all the time. The scale is essentially a Mixolydian scale, but it adds a natural 7th passing tone. In C, this scale spells as C, D, E, F, G, A, B♭, B, C, and its formula in scale degrees is 1, 2, 3, 4, 5, 6, ♭7, 7. Most jazz players will use this over a standard dominant seventh chord (such as C7), and it's important to note that most jazz players play this scale descending only. You can, however, use it any way you want!

The Major Bebop Scale in All Twelve Keys

The next bebop scale is the major bebop scale, and—you guessed it—jazz players like to use this over major chords. It's essentially a major scale, with an additional note between 5 and 6 (a passing tone), to give it the typical chromatic sound that you hear in jazz. In C, the major bebop scale spells as C, D, E, F, G, G♯, A, B, C, and its formula in scale degrees is 1, 2, 3, 4, 5, ♯5, 6, 7.

C Bebop Dominant

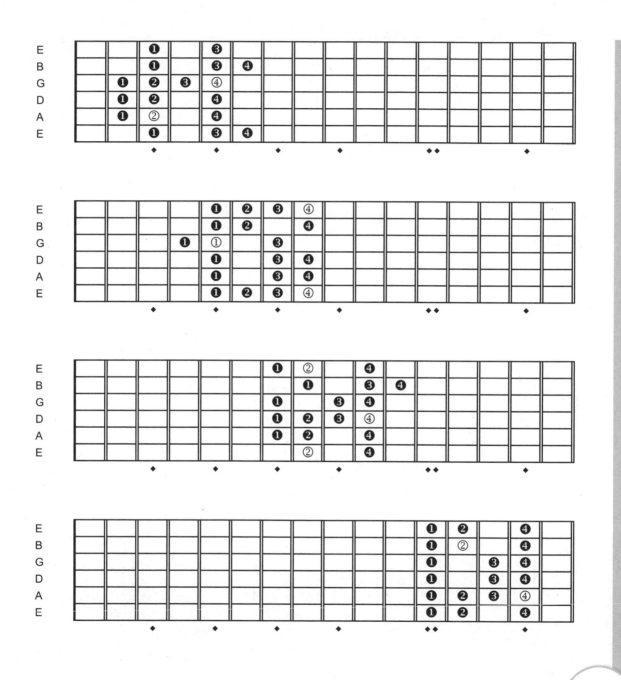

The Bebop Dominant Scale

C#/D♭ Bebop Dominant

The Bebop Dominant Scale

D Bebop Dominant

The Bebop Dominant Scale

D#/E♭ Bebop Dominant

The Bebop Dominant Scale

Track 15

E Bebop Dominant

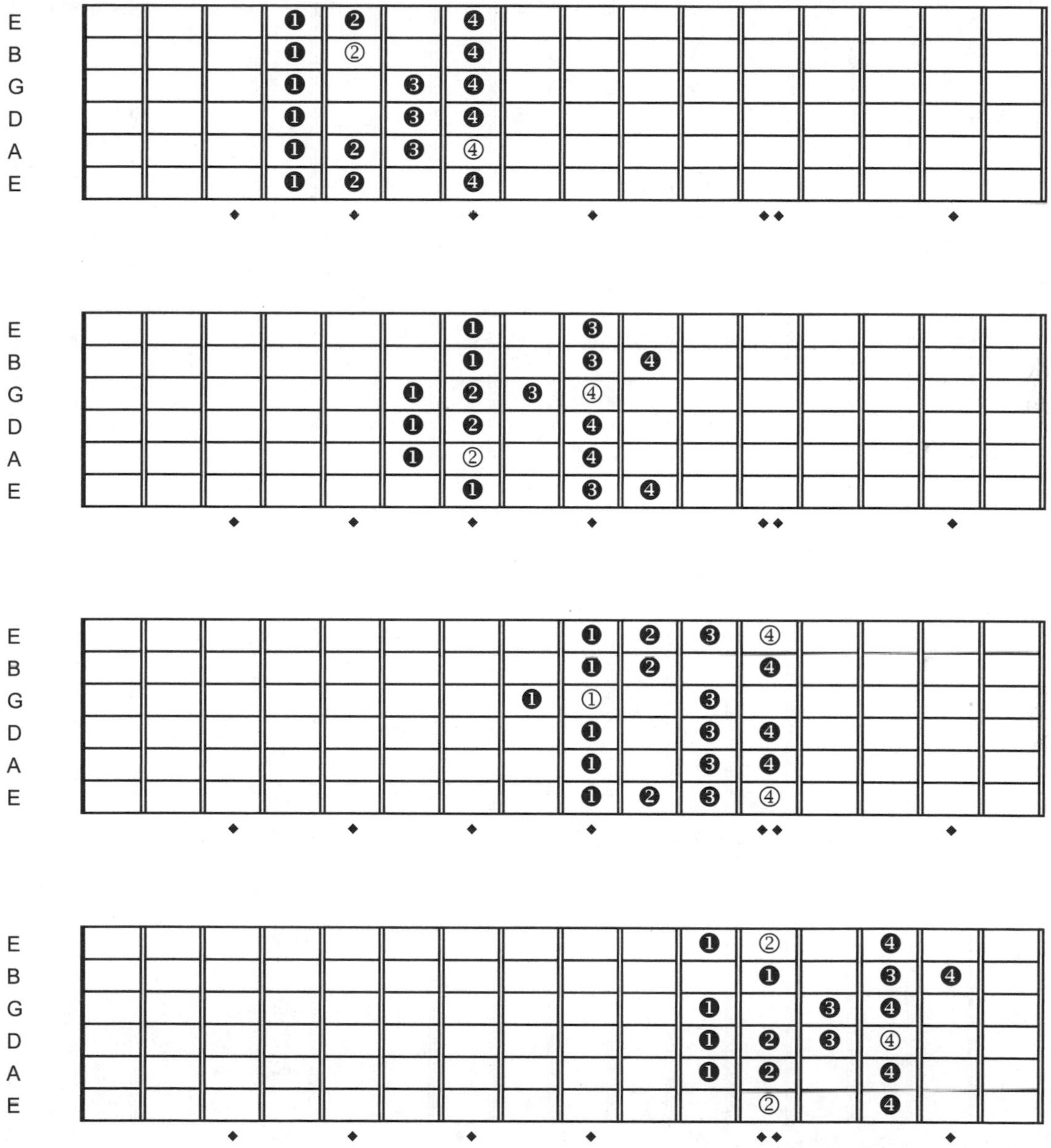

(Right margin, vertical text) **The Bebop Dominant Scale**

F Bebop Dominant

The Bebop Dominant Scale

F♯/G♭ Bebop Dominant

The Bebop Dominant Scale

G Bebop Dominant

The Bebop Dominant Scale

G♯/A♭ Bebop Dominant

A Bebop Dominant

The Bebop Dominant Scale

A#/B♭ Bebop Dominant

B Bebop Dominant

The Bebop Dominant Scale

C Bebop Major

The Major Bebop Scale

C#/D♭ Bebop Major

The Major Bebop Scale

D Bebop Major

The Major Bebop Scale

D#/E♭ Bebop Major

The Major Bebop Scale

Track 16

E Bebop Major

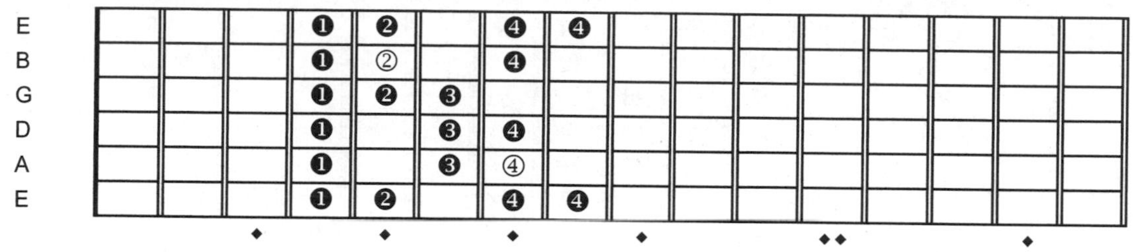

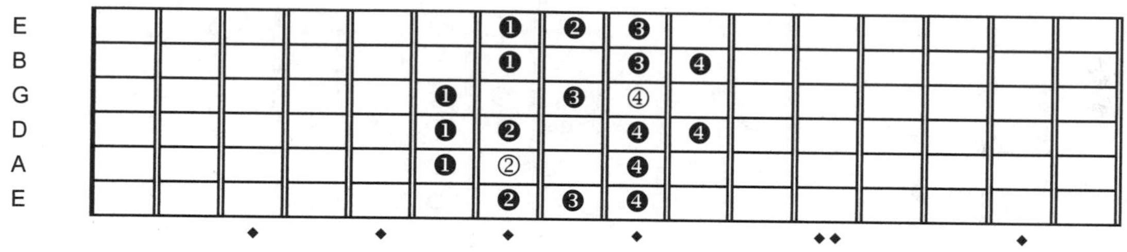

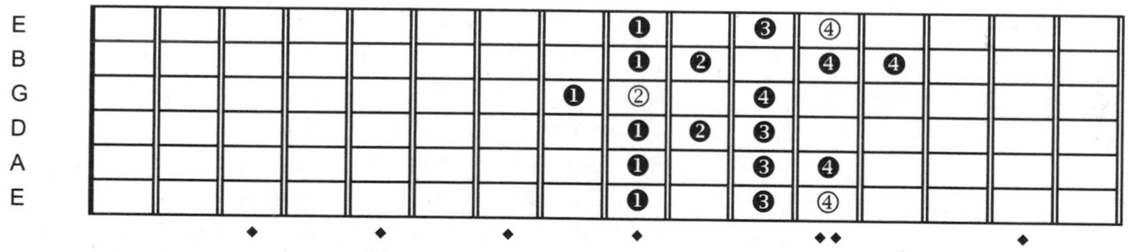

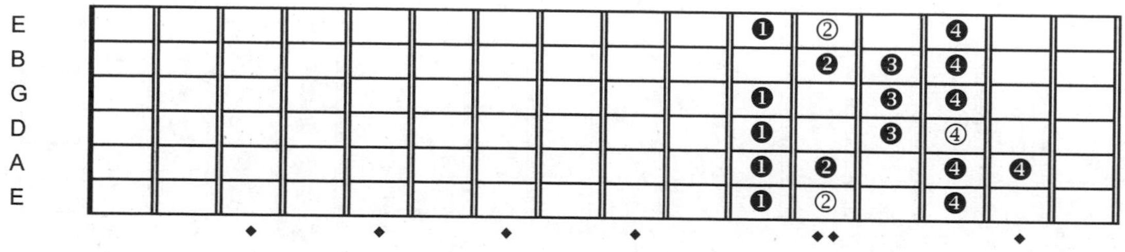

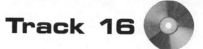

F Bebop Major

The Major Bebop Scale

F#/Gb Bebop Major

G Bebop Major

The Major Bebop Scale

G#/Ab Bebop Major

A Bebop Major

The Major Bebop Scale

A#/B♭ Bebop Major

The Major Bebop Scale

B Bebop Major

The Major Bebop Scale

The Altered Dominant Scale
in All Twelve Keys

In jazz, you're faced with some very odd chords, and no chord or type of chord is mutilated as often as the poor old dominant seventh (such as C7). In a jazz tune, that C7 may appear as a C7#9♭5♭13, and it's totally at the discretion of the pianist playing at the time how "outside" they may push that chord. Of course, when you add odd notes into chords, you're going to need scales that contain those notes in order to make cogent melodies. The altered dominant scale is a scale that contains every possible alteration jazz players put into dominant chords.

In C, the altered dominant scale spells as C, D♭, E♭, E, F#, A♭, B♭, or in scale degrees as 1 ♭2/♭9, ♭3/#9, 3, #4/#11/♭5, #5/♭13, ♭7. When nothing else works, try this scale. It's meant for those impossible dominant chords. Jazz players also love to use this scale over normal dominant chords (that is, unaltered) just to create tension.

The Locrian #2 Scale
in All Twelve Keys

Jazz players deal with the minor7♭5 (half diminished) chord on a regular basis. Normally, the scale of choice is the Locrian mode, but over the years, the dissonance of the Locrian mode gave players the impetus to seek out other scales. By raising the 2nd note of the Locrian mode half a step (it's flat normally in Locrian), many jazz players found a nicer sounding scale over the very prevalent min7♭5 (half diminished) chord. In C, this scale spells as C, D, E♭, F, G♭, A♭, B♭, C, and its interval scale degrees are 1, 2, ♭3, 4, ♭5, ♭6, ♭7. Try this scale out the next time you have to play over a min7♭5 chord—it's a really lovely sound.

C Altered Dominant

The Altered Dominant Scale

C#/D♭ Altered Dominant

D Altered Dominant

The Altered Dominant Scale

D#/E♭ Altered Dominant

The Altered Dominant Scale

Track 17

E Altered Dominant

The Altered Dominant Scale

F Altered Dominant

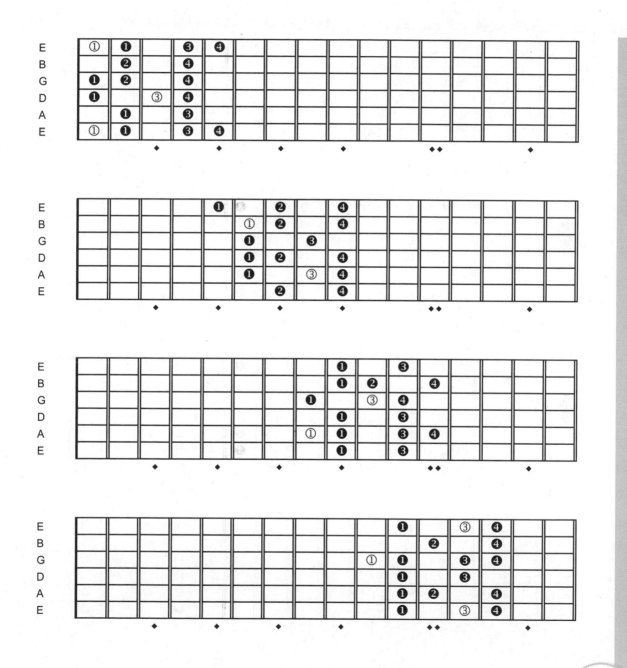

The Altered Dominant Scale

F#/G♭ Altered Dominant

The Altered Dominant Scale

G Altered Dominant

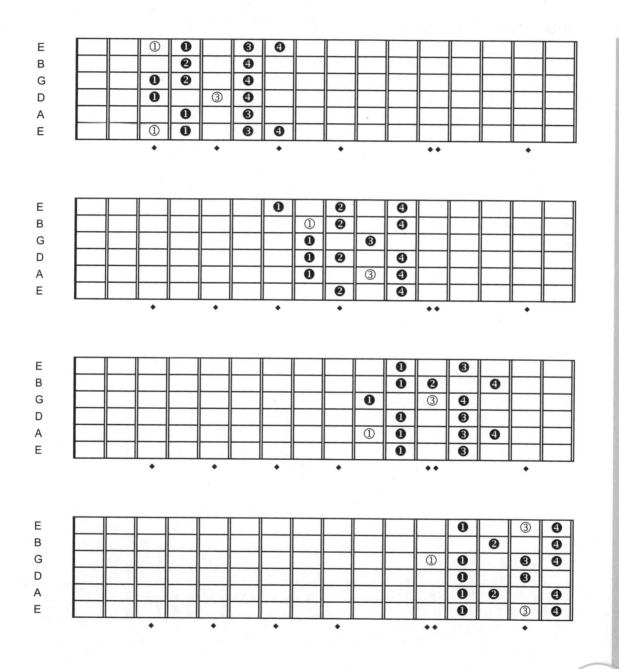

The Altered Dominant Scale

G♯/A♭ Altered Dominant

The Altered Dominant Scale

A Altered Dominant

The Altered Dominant Scale

A#/B♭ Altered Dominant

The Altered Dominant Scale

B Altered Dominant

C Locrian #2

The Locrian #2 Scale

C#/D♭ Locrian #2

D Locrian #2

The Locrian #2 Scale

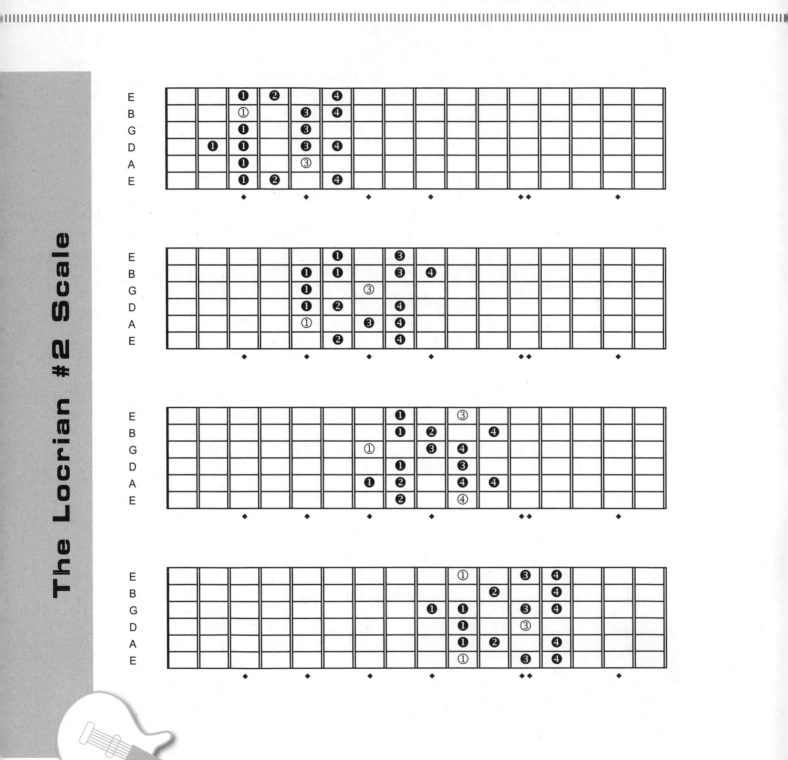

D#/E♭ Locrian #2

The Locrian #2 Scale

 **Track 18**

E Locrian #2

The Locrian #2 Scale

F Locrian #2

The Locrian #2 Scale

F#/G♭ Locrian #2

The Locrian #2 Scale

G Locrian #2

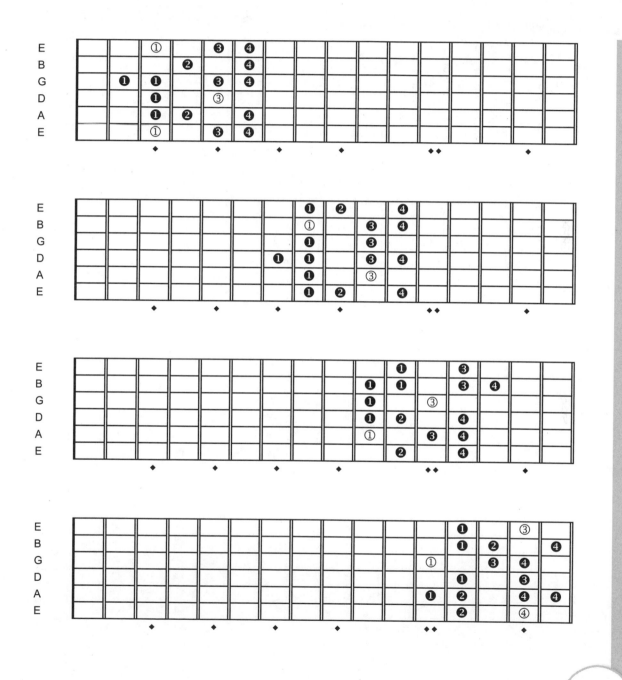

The Locrian #2 Scale

G#/A♭ Locrian #2

The Locrian #2 Scale

A Locrian #2

The Locrian #2 Scale

A#/B♭ Locrian #2

The Locrian #2 Scale

B Locrian #2

The Mixolydian ♯4 Scale in All Twelve Keys

The last scale in this book is the Mixolydian ♯4 scale. Mixolydian scales are used over dominant chords, and in jazz, dominant chords are something special. Sometimes the chords are very plain while at other times they can be very altered. (See the previous section on the altered dominant chord.) What's needed is an in-between sound, something not as plain as Mixolydian, but not as far-out as altered dominant. Along comes the Mixolydian ♯4 scale (another mode of the melodic minor) to bridge the gap.

Many jazz players feel that when you play over a dominant 7th chord, the 4th note of the Mixolydian scale is dissonant. To fix that, you just raise it up half a step. You end up with the Mixolydian ♯4 scale (also called Lydian dominant by some), which spells in C as C, D, E, F♯, G, A, B♭, C. Its interval pattern is 1, 2, 3, ♯4/♯11, 5, 6, ♭7. It's also the best scale to play over a dominant 7♯11 chord (C7♯11). It's a pretty-sounding scale—one that you won't use every day, but when the time is right, there's nothing better.

C Mixolydian #4

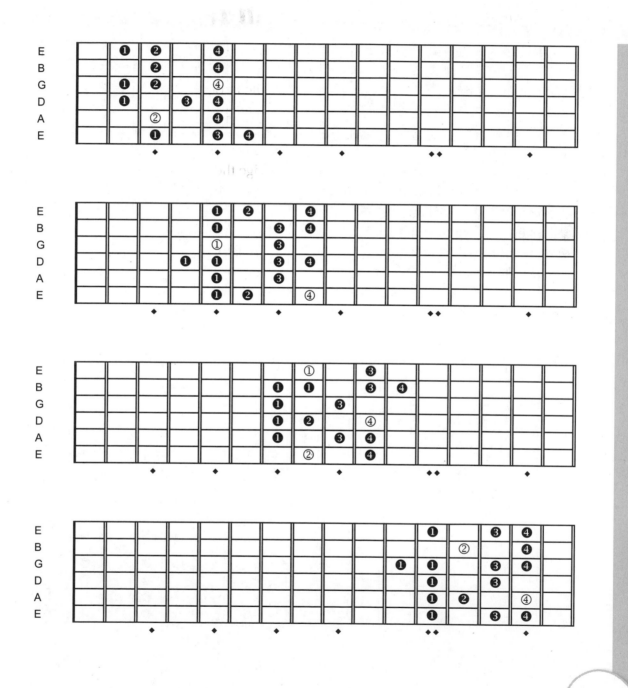

The Mixolydian #4 Scale

The Mixolydian #4 Scale

D Mixolydian #4

The Mixolydian #4 Scale

D♯/E♭ Mixolydian #4

The Mixolydian #4 Scale

Track 19

E Mixolydian #4

The Mixolydian #4 Scale

F Mixolydian #4

The Mixolydian #4 Scale

F#/Gb Mixolydian #4

G Mixolydian #4

The Mixolydian #4 Scale

G♯/A♭ Mixolydian #4

A Mixolydian #4

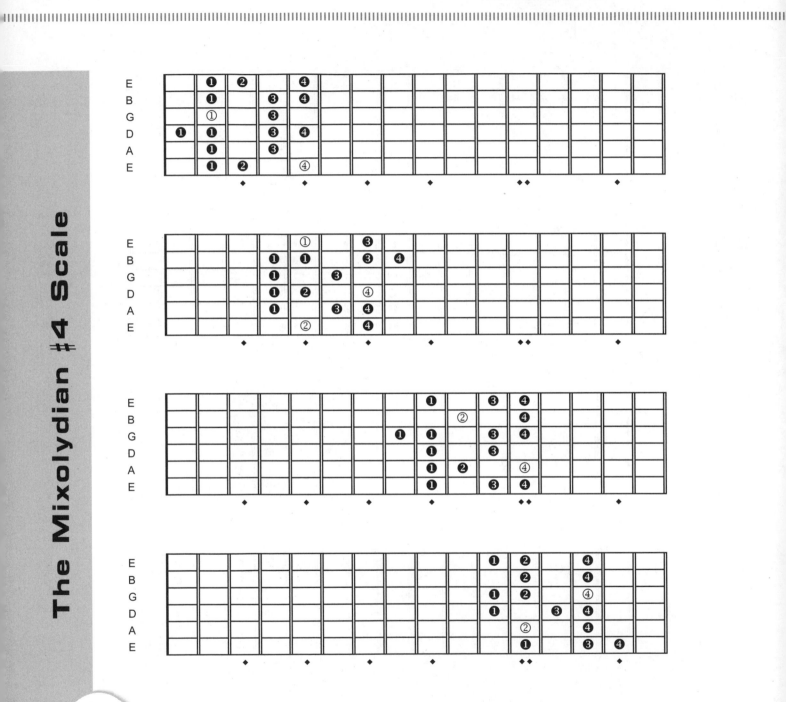

The Mixolydian #4 Scale

A#/B♭ Mixolydian #4

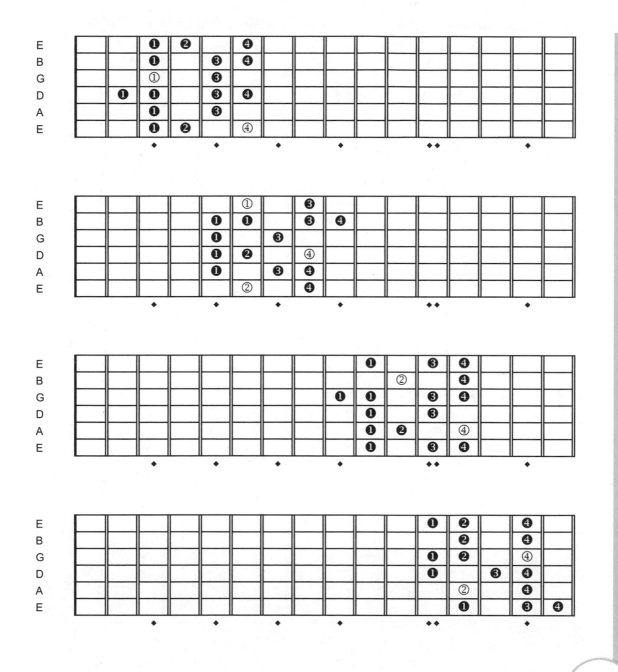

The Mixolydian #4 Scale

B Mixolydian #4

The Mixolydian #4 Scale